• ULTIMATE •
BOOK OF

ADVENTURE

· ULTIMATE ·
BOOK OF

ADVENTURE

*Life-Changing Excursions
and Experiences Around the World*

by Scott McNeely

Illustrations by Arthur Mount

CHRONICLE BOOKS
SAN FRANCISCO

Library of Congress Cataloging-in-Publication Data available.
ISBN 978-1-4521-6422-9

Manufactured in Hong Kong.

MIX
Paper from
responsible sources
FSC™ C136333

Design by Liam Flanagan
Illustrations by Arthur Mount

Chronicle Books LLC
680 Second Street
San Francisco, CA 94107

www.chroniclebooks.com

10 9 8 7 6 5 4 3 2 1

To Aimee, Emmett and Hollis,
and the many adventures yet to come.

CONTENTS

11 Introduction

12 Let's Be Adventurers

13 It's OK to Be Dangerous.
Just Don't Be Stupid.

14 How to Adventure-Hack
Your Life

21 Adventuring with Kids

22 How to Use This Book

25 **Part 1**
ADVENTURES
OF A LIFETIME

27 Track Mountain Gorillas

30 Swim with Humpback Whales

32 Camp with Grizzly Bears

36 Safari on Pack Ice

39 Heli-Ski the Bugaboos

41 Run the Salmon River's
Middle Fork

46 Hang with Hippos

48 Follow the Wildebeest Migration

51 Meet a Mob of Meerkats

54 Get Lost in a Blizzard of Bats

56 Overnight with Emperor
Penguins

59 Trek by Horse in Iceland

62 Dogsled with the Inuit

67 Ride a Camel with Bedouins

69 Travel the Ancient Silk Road

73 Ride the Orient Express

76 Explore the Galápagos Islands

79 Dive with Great White Sharks

83 Hike the Inca Trail

87 Conquer the Lost World

90 Summit Stok Kangri

95 Find Happiness in the Himalayas

98 Drive to the World's End

101 Spend Ten Days in Space

Adventure Skills

35 How to Survive a Bear Attack

44 How to Escape Fast-Moving Water

65 How to Build a Snow Shelter

81 How to Survive a Shark Attack

93 How to Cope with Altitude Sickness

105 **Part 2**
ADVENTURES
FOR ADRENALINE
JUNKIES

107 Surf a Volcano

111 Chase a Tornado

115   Fall to Earth

117   Jump Sky High

119   Train as a Wing Walker

122   Enter the Mongol Rally

126   Run Caballo Blanco

128   Jam in a Hotspot

131   Surf at Mavericks

133   Circle Mont Blanc

135   Fly a Jet Fighter

137   Survive the Sahara

141   Ride the World's Steepest Roller Coaster

142   Try Rodeo Clowning

145   Run with the Bulls

147   Conquer Tough Mudder

149   Bike the Death Road

152   Ultimate Bungee

154   Dive Off a Cliff

156   Kayak Victoria Falls

160   Paraglide with Predators

162   Take a Thrill Walk

164   Defy Earth's Gravity

Adventure Skills

109   How to Treat Cuts and Lacerations

114   How to Survive a Tornado in a Car

125   How to Bribe a Police Officer or Border Guard

139   How to Survive in a Desert

158   How to Survive a Waterfall Plunge

167   **Part 3**

ADVENTURES FOR ODDBALLS

169   Visit Area 51

171   Rock the Air Guitar

173   Plan a Radioactive Holiday

177   Go Zorbing

178   Learn Chessboxing

180   Vacation in a Micronation

183   Join the French Foreign Legion

188   Discover a Lost City

190   Run the Man versus Horse Marathon

192   Ski in the Desert

194   Go Bog Snorkeling

196   Watch a Chukka of Elephant Polo

198   Become a Competitive Eater

201   Ride Your Bike Naked

203   Write a Novel in Thirty Days

205   Join a Circus

208   Have an Urban Adventure

210   Work on a Fishing Boat

215   Volunteer as a Fire Spotter

218   Fake Your Own Kidnapping

223   Race a Rickshaw Across India

225   Start a Tomato Fight

Adventure Skills

175   How to Survive a Nuclear Blast

186   How to Escape from a Prison Camp

213	How to Survive Falling Overboard at Sea
217	How to Survive a Forest Fire
221	How to Evade a Kidnapping Attempt

229 Part 4
ADVENTURES FOR MIND, BODY, AND SPIRIT

231	Send a Note to God
233	Visit the Nazca Lines
236	Retrace the Hippie Trail
238	Perform the Hajj
241	Learn to Firewalk
243	Exercise the Spirit
245	Make the Shikoku Pilgrimage
249	Master the Art of Silence
252	Experience Pure Emptiness
254	Connect with Dreamtime
257	Worship the Sunrise
259	Slow It Way Down
261	Worship in the Temple of Wilderness
266	Move Far from the Madding Crowd
268	Get High with a Shaman
273	Walk the Way of St. James
276	Embrace the Light
278	Get Baptized in India

282	Kora at Mount Kailash
284	Expose Your True Self
287	Commune with the Navajo
290	Book Your Space Funeral

Adventure Skills

248	How to Deal with a Venomous Snake Bite
264	How to Start a Fire in Difficult Conditions
271	How to Survive a Drug Overdose
280	How to Survive a Human Stampede

293 Part 5
ADVENTURE KICK-START GUIDES

295	Visit a World-Class Museum
295	Visit an Oddball Museum
296	Go for a Swim
296	Go Island Hopping
297	Go Scuba Diving
298	Learn a New Talent
298	Tour a Market or Bazaar
299	Get a Massage
300	Learn to Cook
300	Visit a Craft Brewery
301	Worship a Sports Stadium
302	Gamble in Style
302	Play a Round of Golf
303	Expose Yourself to Public Art

INTRODUCTION

Compared to any other time in human history, we've got it good.

Most of us live long and healthy lives. Food is plentiful. Technology keeps us connected. We have doctors to cure our ills and scientists to teach us about the universe. Everything is by no means perfect, yet in the great arc of human history, we live in a golden age.

And it's all a little boring, isn't it?

Modern life, for all its conveniences, insulates us from adventure. We shop online, binge-watch television, and relentlessly check social media. We don't bother using all our vacation time. We worry. We overthink. We shy away from risk. We close ourselves off to what we do not already know. Far too many of us prize predictability and the familiar over the rough and bumpy road of the unknown.

Hopefully this book will change that. Of course, I don't expect you to attempt every adventure within these covers. But try at least one. Go outside your comfort zone. If you're a planner, throw away the plan. If you're a nonplanner, get yourself organized. Either way, be open to the new and different. Be open to having an honest-to-goodness *adventure*.

Why? Because we are all better off being adventurous. To live a rewarding life means taking risks. Trying something unfamiliar. Doing a familiar thing differently. Pursuing a new experience or skill no matter how uncomfortable it feels.

And no, it doesn't matter what you do or where you go. All that matters is waking up, unsure of what the day may bring. Your adventure starts when you embrace that uncomfortable—and exhilarating—sense of possibility.

SCOTT McNEELY

LET'S BE ADVENTURERS

For most of human history, adventure wasn't something you had to look for. Adventure found *you*.

Back in *ye olden days*, you might have been chased by lions across the plains of Africa or have your village unexpectedly ransacked by barbarians. You might have had your caravan robbed, or your castle sieged, or your city struck by a deadly plague.

Or perhaps you were an explorer. You set sail on a grand voyage of exploration on a Viking longboat, or in a Chinese junk boat, or in Irish fishing currach. You chartered a rough course and set sail with hope—but no guarantee—of a safe return home.

Adventurers can sweep aside the conventions of their time in pursuit of knowledge and self-discovery. They seek adrenaline rushes to jolt them into feeling alive, and they make pilgrimages in pursuit of the divine hiding in plain sight here on Earth.

Participating in unusual and exciting, and often hazardous, experiences—that's the dictionary definition of *adventure* and good enough as far as definitions go. Just keep in mind, adventures come in many shapes and sizes. There are many paths leading to the doorstep of adventure, and there is no wrong or right way to have one. There are only two things you need: an openness to new experiences and the courage to go and do it.

The hardest part is making the decision to go. The rest is easy.

IT'S OK TO BE DANGEROUS.
JUST DON'T BE STUPID.

Somebody once said, "To risk is to live."

While it is not a bad bumper sticker for life, it does not mean that adventures must always be life-threatening. There is no need to take crazy risks. Nobody wants a misadventure, and nobody wants to die.

That said, there is no getting around the fact that many activities covered in this book are dangerous. Some activities—yeah, we're talking about you, BASE jumping!—are downright insane. Your chances of being seriously injured or dying as a result of taking part in many activities in this book are uncomfortably high.

It goes without saying that you are putting both your health and life at risk, and it is your responsibility to be responsible. Know your limits. Don't take unnecessary risks. And be aware that something can go wrong—the weather, your health, your equipment—and usually does. You must be prepared to deal with changing conditions. Your life may literally depend upon it.

Medical insurance? Emergency evacuation coverage? Accidental death and dismemberment? Don't roll your eyes. If you get stuck on the side of a mountain and need urgent medical care, who will provide it and how will you pay for it? It's smart to purchase travel-specific health coverage wherever you go to cover the costs of unexpected medical issues. Many plans include emergency evacuation coverage to ensure you receive urgent care in a timely manner.

Before you leave on a trip, it's also important to consult with your doctor, and complete any recommended vaccinations. You have only one body. Treat it well.

HOW TO ADVENTURE-HACK YOUR LIFE

How can I do this? I could never afford it. I'm still in school. I've just finished school. I've got a job. I'm quitting a job. I've got kids. I've got too many bills to pay. I am getting too damn old. I don't know where to go or what to do. . . .

Sometimes we all need help and a little encouragement.

Fortunately, many organizations and agencies exist with the sole purpose of helping people like you have unforgettable adventures. It doesn't matter if you're in high school or retired, if you're single or married with kids—there's an adventure out there with your name on it.

Gap Year

A gap year is typically a break between high school and college. While it doesn't need to last a full year, it does need to last more than a week or two. That's the difference between a mere *vacation* and a true learning *experience*, which is what gap years are meant to be.

Studies show that for some students, a gap year better prepares them for absorbing the educational and life lessons offered in a college curriculum. It gives students time to mature, to become a little less "me, me, me!" and a little more aware of the world and others in it.

On the downside, gap years can seem like an expensive boondoggle. Not all kids can handle the unstructured time away from home—which is a likely sign that they aren't ready for college life, either.

A good compromise, perhaps, is an official gap year program. Numerous educational and nonprofit agencies have excellent half- and full-year programs. Some are vocational in nature (au pair abroad, learn yoga, etc.) while others are mission-based with a focus on do-gooding (spend a year in Africa, work with needy families, etc.).

No matter what, gap years can be life-changing. Spending time abroad in the late teenage years, and getting a chance to live and learn in a foreign culture, are key ingredients for nurturing creative and open minds. These traits, in turn, will unlock a life full of adventure.

Study Abroad

The belief is that by a student's junior year of college, he or she can reap a lifetime of benefit by completing one year of study at a foreign college or university.

Academics are important, of course. But the driving force for studying abroad is more social and cultural in nature: socializing with people who grew up in different cultures, potentially speaking a different language, and being exposed to different religions, political systems, and perspectives on the world. Plus, there's the added benefit of living in a foreign country, with opportunities for travel and even short-term work.

Study abroad programs come in all shapes and sizes, in hundreds of countries. It can be overwhelming sorting through the many and dizzying options.

Programs typically last for a semester or a full year. Competition for international students is fierce, often because of the money and prestige that come to foreign universities as a result of hosting American students. Shop carefully, compare the different offers, and look for programs that cater to a well-balanced educational experience both in and outside the classroom.

Teach Abroad

Get paid to teach and explore a new culture while living abroad?! For many people, teaching abroad is a dream come true.

Numerous programs place university graduates in paid teaching positions around the world, often with a strong emphasis on teaching English-language skills in foreign public schools, private international schools, colleges, universities, and ESL (English as a Second Language) schools.

You'll make a difference in others' lives, gain real-world working experience, and have numerous opportunities to travel. Most teachers earn enough to save a few hundred dollars per month after expenses. Schools prefer to employ citizens of native English-speaking nations. A four-year degree (typically a bachelor's degree) is required, often in addition to an accredited TEFL (Teaching English as a Foreign Language) or TESOL (Teaching English to Speakers of Other Languages) certification. Certification can be done in person (typically a month of part-time coursework) or online (usually three to six months).

Countries such as Vietnam, China, Thailand, Malaysia, and South Korea have many well-paid openings for foreign English teachers. Positions are also available in Eastern Europe, Central and South America, and many African countries.

Volunteer Abroad

You can volunteer your time and energy in two ways.

First, through service organizations in the United States (AmeriCorps and Senior Corps) and internationally (Peace Corps,

Red Cross, Habitat for Humanity, Doctors Without Borders). These are networks of programs that, depending upon your interests and availability, determine which program is best for you.

Service commitments vary from three months (a summer program) to one or two years. Most programs require a full-time commitment, though it is possible to find part-time service opportunities. Volunteers typically receive a living allowance to cover basic expenses.

The second option is a volunteer vacation. These short-term programs, usually one to three weeks, focus on assisting established programs in developing countries. The idea is to encourage people who cannot commit to a long-term service program, but who still want to make a difference in the world and are willing to give back in any way they can.

These programs are often fee based, which means *you* pay to volunteer. While it may sound unfair or even shady to pay, the reality is most programs cannot easily accommodate an influx of short-term volunteers. Programs charge a fee to cover the costs of finding and providing accommodation and useful projects for vacation volunteers. You may spend a week or two supporting local families in need with day care, elder care, or youth tutoring, and generally helping to serve the needs of the local community.

Work Abroad

Most work-abroad programs are in the hospitality industry and customer service. The idea is to pay for your travels by spending a few months working in industries that prize English-speaking staff.

Amusement parks, resorts, and cruise lines commonly offer three- to six-month contracts, and often handle the visa and paperwork requirements for you. Positions in restaurants, bars, youth hostels and hotels, and small-scale organic farms offer shorter contracts.

Most countries require special visas to work and earn income. It's possible to apply independently for a work visa. Also consider a reputable work-abroad agency, which vets the positions and companies and can support you if things don't work out as expected.

Career Break

More and more companies are offering formal sabbatical programs to employees. It's a way to retain quality staff and offer tangible rewards for dedication to the organization. Typical programs are available after seven to ten years of full-time employment. Sabbaticals last anywhere from three to six months—sometimes even more! There are usually no strings attached to how you spend your time on sabbatical: travel, hang out with family, learn a new skill, start a band, become a painter, do nothing at all, it's really up to you.

The best sabbatical programs pay 100 percent of your salary while you're away. All programs guarantee your job upon return.

Another option is to plan for an extended break whenever you leave your current job. This is not easy. It requires courage, for example, to quit a well-paying job in order to take a year's break (or longer). Health insurance, rent, mortgages, car payments, school loans—there are a million reasons why career breaks are frightening. But the benefits are real: Studies show that people who take career breaks live longer and healthier lives, experience fewer divorces, and tend to score highest on quality-of-life surveys.

If your break includes developing an existing skill or learning a new one, even better.

Home Swaps & House Sitting

Got a house or apartment? Then you can save hundreds, possibly thousands, of dollars when you travel. The idea is to vacation in someone else's home while they (sometimes) stay in yours. It saves money and, from an adventuring perspective, can mean a more local and authentic experience. When you stay in nontouristy neighborhoods and live like locals do, you're well on your way to having a more engaging travel experience.

Dozens of agencies intermediate between home and apartment swappers, vetting applications, and making home and neighborhood recommendations based on personalization algorithms and social media data. Sites specialize in one of three areas, so know which one makes the most sense for you: a simultaneous home swap (you stay in their home, they stay in yours), a nonsimultaneous exchange (you stay in somebody's second home), or a hospitality exchange where you stay in somebody's house while they're also in the house (think Airbnb, Couchsurfing, and similar peer-to-peer rental services).

House sitting, on the other hand, is an option for people who are prepared to take care of someone's home (and often their pets) in exchange for a free place to stay. Of course, it's not really free. Caring for someone's home and their pets is a major responsibility and requires a significant time commitment. Still, it's a good option for a few weeks, giving you a base while exploring a new city on the cheap.

Round-the-World Travel

A "round the world" (RTW) ticket is an excellent way to save on travel costs and to extend your itinerary to cover as much of the globe as possible. RTW tickets allow multiple stops in multiple countries, typically leveraging the network of an airline alliance such as Oneworld (including British Airways, Qantas, and American Airlines), Star Alliance (including United Airlines, Lufthansa, and Air India), and SkyTeam (including Delta Air Lines, Air France, and Virgin Atlantic).

Each alliance offers a variety of RTW options. Oneworld, for example, offers a straightforward continent-based fare (Oneworld Explorer) or a more versatile distance-based fare (Global Explorer). The latter allows you to fly up to 26,000 miles with up to sixteen stops en route. RTW tickets cost between $1,500 and $10,000, depending on your total mileage, the routes, and total number of stops.

You can often use frequent-flier points to purchase RTW tickets. In fact, savvy travelers can literally travel the world, for free, using nothing but miles and points. It's completely legal. It just takes hard work and proper planning.

The trick is earning as many airline frequent-flier and hotel points as possible, without buying anything outside of what you would normally purchase. Start with an airline or hotel credit card: You can potentially earn fifty thousand points for simply signing up, ten thousand points for your first purchase, plus an additional hundred thousand points if you spend, say, more than $2,500 in the first six months. Boom! An offer like that is too good to pass up. So go ahead, prepay your car insurance, buy all your groceries on the card, and maybe even pay your rent, too! You'll earn the bonus with ease.

ADVENTURING WITH KIDS

The first rule of traveling with kids is: Do not think too hard. There's never a right time to travel with kids. It's always tough. Somebody is always sick. Somebody is always a crankypants. It doesn't matter. Traveling as a family is simply more fun, and after a few days you'll be surprised at how easy it actually is, and how much everybody is enjoying it.

Keep in mind that newborns can travel, too. You can breastfeed in Paris or Bangkok just as easily as on the couch back home. You're not sleeping much with a newborn, anyway, so what's a little jet lag?

Also remember that toddlers, in particular, are easier to manage outside than inside. Trade your house or apartment for low-key camping or trekking—walk the streets of a new city, explore the parks and attractions with your kid in tow. Everybody will love it, as long as you do not overschedule the family and do not try to see too much.

When the kids get older, consider a family volunteer vacation. Families of all ages and sizes can experience a different culture and work together to help others in a meaningful way. It's fun, boosts kids' confidence, and creates lots of strong, shared memories.

If the idea of volunteering is appealing to your teen, consider a volunteer program specifically tailored for high school students. These programs are often in a group volunteer camp with other teenagers and take place during spring, winter, and summer breaks.

HOW TO USE THIS BOOK

First off, a word of warning: Many of the activities in this book are genuinely dangerous things to do. Your health and life may be at risk, so approach every adventure in this book with an appropriate amount of caution. Do your own research before attempting any of these activities.

That said, every adventure in this book is meant to be an activity that *you*, the person holding this book right now, can actually do. Granted, few of us have $50 million to spend on a ten-day voyage to the International Space Station or want to risk our lives in so many different ways. Yet the amazing thing is, you *can* do these things, if you possess both the desire and the money.

Speaking of money, to assist in your budgeting and planning, each adventure includes a rough estimate of cost using the following scale:

$	Less than $500
$$	Between $500 and $1,500
$$$	Between $1,500 and $3,000
$$$$	Between $3,000 and $5,000
$$$$$	More than $5,000

Each adventure also includes a "Physical Difficulty" rating based on the following scale:

LOW	Feasible for people in decent health
MEDIUM	Requires moderate physical exertion; you'll likely sweat and have a few aches and pains when it's all over.

| HIGH | Only for fit people who can handle an intense physical experience that may include severe conditions and extreme temperatures. |
| EXTREME | For experts only. Don't try this at home. |

And then—not to bum you out—there is the "Likelihood to Die" rating. It's intended to illuminate the underlying inherent risks involved in taking part in these adventures. The scale is:

LOW	Relax, you'll make it.
MEDIUM	The odds of dying here are *not* zero. Pay attention.
HIGH	Your chances of being seriously injured or dying are uncomfortably high.
EXTREME	No joke; people pursuing this activity have been permanently disfigured, seriously injured, or killed. Experts only.

Finally, there is the "Brag Factor," which rates how envious your friends will be. Think of it as the pride-o-meter, or how much you may impress fellow adventurers by participating in the activity. The scale is:

LOW	It's a cool thing to do and you're in good company. Many others have done it.
MEDIUM	Others have done it, but not many. You'll have a great story to tell at parties.
HIGH	You're a true adventurer, and among the elite few to have accomplished this amazing feat. You'll be talking about this for years to come.
EXTREME	VIP adventurers only. People know your name, you're *that* famous of an adventurer.

Adventures of a Lifetime

——— —— —— ———

*Twenty-four experiences
with the potential to change
your life. You only live once,
so let the adventures begin.*

TRACK MOUNTAIN GORILLAS

WHAT Meet the world's last wild mountain gorillas
WHERE Volcanoes National Park, Rwanda
BRAG FACTOR Medium
LIKELIHOOD TO DIE Low
BEST TIME TO GO June–September or late December–February
PHYSICAL DIFFICULTY High
COST $$$$

There are fewer than nine hundred mountain gorillas left on Earth. Let that sink in for a moment.

Gorillas provoke us to ask deep questions about the nature of human intelligence and language. Staring into the eyes of a gorilla is as mesmerizing as it is discomfiting: You are peering into the humanlike eyes of a distant relative. And yet, fewer than nine hundred of these majestic mountain creatures remain.

Mountain gorillas are the species made famous by zoologist Dian Fossey in her memoir, *Gorillas in the Mist*. They are also huge stars in movies like *King Kong*. Mountain gorillas are critically endangered—the last remaining pockets (none live in zoos) are in the remote border areas between Uganda, Rwanda, and the Democratic Republic of the Congo (DRC).

All three countries offer gorilla trekking. It's the most expensive in Rwanda, but in exchange for the higher fees you get easier access (less than three hours from Kigali on decent roads), better visibility (the vegetation in Uganda and the DRC is denser), and treks that are less physically demanding, especially given the relatively large population of mountain gorillas—more than three hundred at last count—that live in Rwanda's Volcanoes National Park.

Plus, Rwanda itself is an intriguing travel destination. Since the tragic genocide that occurred in the country in the mid-1990s, Rwanda has begun the process of healing both its people and its lands. Rwanda is considered safe to visit. And with numerous conservation efforts in and around places like the stunning Lake Kivu, Rwanda is about a lot more than gorillas. Though, of course, gorillas are what bring in the much-needed tourism dollars.

The Basics

Gorilla trekking is not easy, and it requires more physical exertion than your standard animal safari. The altitude ranges from a low of about 5,000 feet to a high of about 10,000 feet over steep mountain passes.

In Rwanda's Volcanoes National Park, visitors are allowed to track one of ten groups ranging in size from a dozen gorillas to more than forty. The gorillas move frequently, which mean hikes can take anywhere from one to six hours each way to reach a gorilla group. You'll be assigned a trekking group based on your personal fitness level.

Trackers throughout the park keep tabs on each gorilla group. Your guide will know roughly where to go. Once you find your assigned gorilla group, you have sixty minutes to observe the animals. In Rwanda, fewer than eighty individual trekking permits are issued daily, and each trekking group is limited to eight people.

Exposure to humans is minimized to protect the animals. It also means the treks are expensive; permits alone cost $750 per person, with two- or three-day tours including accommodation from $1,250 and up. It's common to prebook treks to lock in dates, obtain a permit, and provide transport to and from Kigali, Rwanda's capital. Volcanoes National Park is a two-and-a-half-hour drive on paved roads from Kigali's international airport.

While gorilla treks are offered year-round, the best time to go is during one of Rwanda's two dry seasons: June to September or late December to February.

THINGS TO KNOW

- × Children under the age of fifteen are not allowed on gorilla treks in Rwanda.

- × Do not trek with gorillas if you have a cold, a fever, or the flu. Gorillas and humans are closely related—we can swap viruses—but do not share the same immune system. Gorillas are at risk if they contract a human disease.

- × Hire a porter. They congregate near the park entrance and, for a nominal fee of $10, carry bags and assist as needed. Even if you don't need the help, hiring a porter is beneficial to the overall gorilla conservation effort. Many porters are reformed ex-poachers.

TRUE OR FALSE? Humans and gorillas are more closely related than horses and zebras.

True. Humans and gorillas share more than 98.6% of the DNA in our genes, slightly more than horses and zebras.

SWIM WITH HUMPBACK WHALES

WHAT Take a dip with hundreds of baby whales
WHERE Vava'u, Tonga
BRAG FACTOR Medium
LIKELIHOOD TO DIE Low
PHYSICAL DIFFICULTY Low
BEST TIME TO GO July–October
COST $$–$$$

Gentle giants. It's counterintuitive to think that one of Earth's largest creatures is also one of the most gentle, and yet it's true.

The "gentle" reputation comes from their behavior. Humpbacks don't bite (they don't have teeth) and are generally nonthreatening filter feeders. They sing haunting songs over vast distances. They jump acrobatically in the air, possibly just for the fun of it. Mothers travel thousands of miles alongside their young, nursing the calves with milk just like any good mammalian mother would.

Tonga is one of the few places in the world where you can reliably swim with humpback whales. Each year, hundreds of humpback pods migrate from the cold and protein-rich waters of Antarctica to Tonga's warm and reef-protected tropical waters to mate and give birth.

The Basics

The remote island group of Vava'u is roughly 200 miles north of Tongatapu, Tonga's main island and the location of its international airport and capital city, Nuku'alofa. Vava'u's distant location keeps visitors to a minimum. You must be motivated to visit.

From July through October, when the humpbacks arrive and give birth, a few dozen licensed operators run sightseeing and swimming excursions with the whales, taking care not to intrude too closely. Multiday packages, including air transfers and accommodations as well as swimming with the whales, cost $1,000 and up.

Multiday liveaboards are also popular, combining whale swims with reef dives (diving in Vava'u and throughout Tonga is generally excellent).

THINGS TO KNOW

- While humpback whales are not the largest creatures on Earth (that's the blue whale), they are definitely in the top ten. Females humpbacks are generally larger than males.

- In Tonga, you can swim with humpback whales every day except Sunday. It's a compulsory rest day in Tonga. No activities!

- Humpbacks return to Vava'u on a roughly eleven-month cycle, which is the amount of time a baby humpback gestates.

- Mature female humpbacks give birth every two to three years and prefer doing so in warm, reef-protected waters. It's the reason why the humpbacks return each year to Vava'u.

- Tonga is the only monarchy in the Pacific and the only Pacific nation to never lose its indigenous government. Its total population is just over one hundred thousand people, spread across forty-eight islands.

TRUE OR FALSE? Humpback whales never sleep.

Mostly true. Unlike humans, humpbacks are so-called conscious breathers, which means they must remember to breathe even while asleep. As a result, sleeping humpbacks only switch off one side of their brain at a time. In human terms, it's more like dozing than sleeping.

CAMP WITH GRIZZLY BEARS

WHAT Get up close and personal with grizzly bears
WHERE McNeil River, Alaska
BRAG FACTOR High
LIKELIHOOD TO DIE Low
BEST TIME TO GO July–Aug
PHYSICAL DIFFICULTY Medium
COST $$–$$$

Alaska's McNeil River State Game Sanctuary and Refuge is one of the few places on Earth where you can sit within a stone's throw of wild grizzly bears and watch them hunt, nap, play, fight, and do everything else that comes naturally.

The sanctuary protects about 200 square miles of pristine Alaskan wilderness. It's beautiful, to be sure, but what draws people in are the wild bears. They gather each year in the hundreds to chomp on summer runs of calico-patterned chum salmon from the Mikfik Creek and the nearby McNeil River.

Mighty Alaskan brown bears—the same species as grizzly bears, just darker and larger—hook salmon after salmon, gorging themselves and flinging mauled carcasses, all within a few yards of humans armed with little more than cameras and GoPros. The bears are completely oblivious to the human bystanders. It's what makes this such a unique wildlife-viewing experience.

Brown bears are usually solitary creatures. However, each year in early July and through mid-August, dozens of bears congregate around the banks of McNeil Falls and its pools, which are teeming with salmon heading upstream to spawning grounds. A lucky few—no more than ten people per day—are allowed to quietly observe.

The Basics

The McNeil River State Game Sanctuary is not a resort. This is a roadless area with no amenities. There are no restaurants or hotels. You sleep on the ground, you pack your own food, and you cook all your meals.

Every morning for four days you hike 2 miles from the camping area down to the river. You spend all day (six to ten hours) watching bears and, in the late afternoon, you return to base camp. It's a simple routine that maximizes both safety and your time with the bears.

McNeil River is so popular that permits are awarded by lottery. The Alaska Department of Fish and Game limits the number of people who can be present at McNeil River Falls and the adjacent viewing areas to a maximum of ten people per day between June 7 and August 25. The area is closed at all other times. Permit applications are due online by March 1; lottery winners are notified in mid-March.

If selected in the lottery, you pay $350 per person (four people maximum per application) and pick a four-day time block for bear viewing. There are no age restrictions for visiting the sanctuary, but think twice before bringing young children.

Access to McNeil River is generally by floatplane from Homer, Kenai, or Anchorage. Expect to pay $800 and up for round-trip air service to McNeil.

THINGS TO KNOW

- × Brown bears are dangerous. The bears at McNeil are neither tame nor friendly. They ignore you simply because you are not a threat.

- × As many as 144 individual bears have been observed at McNeil River through the summer, with as many as 74 bears observed at one time.

× No one has ever been injured by a bear at McNeil River. To preserve that perfect safety record, all visitors in bear-viewing areas are accompanied by armed park rangers.

TRUE OR FALSE? It's possible to gain the trust of a wild Alaskan brown bear.

False. Timothy Treadwell tried. He lived with bears for thirteen summers in Alaska's Katmai National Park. Unfortunately, in 2003, he and his girlfriend were mauled to death and eaten. Filmmaker Werner Herzog used much of Treadwell's first-hand footage, as well as brutal audio recordings of the bear attack, in the 2005 documentary Grizzly Man.

Adventure Skill

HOW TO SURVIVE A BEAR ATTACK

BASIC

Avoid making eye contact. It's often perceived by bears as a threat and can provoke them to attack.

Don't climb a tree. All bears are excellent climbers.

Don't run. You cannot outrun a bear. More likely, it will assume you are prey and chase you down.

Carry pepper spray. Bear-specific brands (do not use human or dog varieties) stream a cloud of concentrated capsaicin spray for eight seconds, over distances of up to 20 feet. It will stop a bear in its tracks, as long as your aim is true.

ADVANCED

Stand your ground. Bears will often charge to see what you will do. Stay perfectly still when a bear is charging you.

With black bears, make noise and fight back. Black bears may be deterred by large and loud responses. In the unlikely event of an attack, use fists and rocks to pummel the bear, especially around the face. Black bears often give up rather than fight.

With grizzly or brown bears, drop to the ground in the fetal position, cover the back of your neck, and play dead. Grizzlies may stop attacking once they feel you are not a threat.

Once an attacking bear loses interest, continue to play dead. Do not get up or move, even if you are injured. Grizzlies, in particular, may wait in the distance to see if you get back up.

If a bear is stalking you, it's the sign of an imminent predatory attack. Likely the bear is hungry. Fighting is your only option.

SAFARI ON PACK ICE

WHAT There's no better way to see polar bears in the wild
WHERE Svalbard, Norway
BRAG FACTOR Medium
LIKELIHOOD TO DIE Low
PHYSICAL DIFFICULTY Medium
BEST TIME TO GO May–September
COST $$–$$$$

Most people have never heard of Svalbard. It's a remote archipelago just inside the Arctic Circle, closer to the North Pole than to mainland Norway.

Svalbard is the sort of place that is dark and forbidding in winter, sunless for months at a time, a rugged terrain of glaciers, fjords, and endless tundra. Summer brings out the sun, which shines twenty-four hours a day, and a rare few months to track the Arctic's most ferocious predator, the polar bear.

Svalbard is not a wildlife refuge, yet its remote location and minimal human footprint (fewer than 2,900 people live here) mean there is little to disrupt the polar bear's way of life. The local bear population is thriving. More than three thousand polar bears call the region home, a number that is healthy and has actually increased in the past two decades, unlike in other parts of the fast-warming Arctic.

Polar bear safaris typically involve a few days on a ship, sailing up Svalbard's remote coast and making forays by dinghy or kayak into iceberg-dotted fjords, hunting for signs of polar bears, walruses, seals, arctic foxes, and reindeer.

Polar bear sightings are always thrilling. They weigh nearly a thousand pounds. They can run at speeds in excess of 25 miles per hour. They stand nearly 8 feet tall. And they can hold their breath underwater for three minutes as they hunt unsuspecting seals lounging on ice floes.

In fact, you're most likely to see a polar bear hunting for seals on the pack ice, sometimes within just a few hundred yards of your ship.

The Basics

Polar bears are wild animals and strongly protected under Norwegian law. Land-based safaris are generally not allowed. The best way to encounter polar bears in the wild is on a multiday cruise from Spitsbergen, the only permanently populated island in Svalbard.

The most important decisions you need to make are how long (day trip or multiday) and what size of ship (large or small). From Spitsbergen, multiday cruises on smaller vessels (twelve to twenty passengers) head north and east into the archipelago's remote reaches and virtually guarantee multiple polar-bear sightings. Expect to pay $4,500 and up for a typical seven-day itinerary.

Larger ships tend to make shorter cruises. They cost less, no more than $200 per person, but polar bear sightings are hit-or-miss.

It's cold in Svalbard, even in summer. Daytime temperatures average in the low 20 degrees Fahrenheit, dropping to zero or below at night. Never forget you're in the Arctic!

THINGS TO KNOW

- × Polar bears are the largest bear species on Earth. No offense, grizzly bears, but polar bears are more aggressive and can probably beat you in a fight. Just sayin'.

- × Speaking of fights, the polar bear's only natural predator besides humans is the killer whale. Epic battles between them have been captured on video.

- × Polar bears are superb swimmers and can swim for miles at a time, if needed.

- × When you're traveling in Svalbard's polar-bear territory, you are legally *required* to carry polar bear deterrents, usually a signal pistol that makes a loud noise.

- × Locals are *required* to carry and know how to use a high-powered rifle anytime they leave Svalbard's few settlements.

TRUE OR FALSE? It is illegal to die in Svalbard.

Kinda sorta. It's more accurate to say it's illegal to be buried in Svalbard. That's because there's only one graveyard on the island and it stopped accepting new burials years ago due to a lack of decomposition. Permafrost prevents bodies from decaying. Gross. The government kindly requires you to die someplace else.

HELI-SKI THE BUGABOOS

WHAT Soar, rip, repeat
WHERE British Columbia, Canada
BRAG FACTOR Medium
LIKELIHOOD TO DIE Low
BEST TIME TO GO December–March
PHYSICAL DIFFICULTY Medium
COST $$$$–$$$$$

They come for one reason: fresh, untracked powder.

And here the powder comes with a spectacular twist. There are no ski lifts. No snow cats. No rope pulls. This is powder skiing by helicopter!

Heli-skiing for the first time is unbelievably cool. Carving smooth turns down a few thousand vertical feet of untouched powder. The intense stillness of the backcountry. Senses humming from the rush of the helicopter flight, soaring deep into canyons and valleys searching for the next run. If you've never skied or snowboarded by helicopter, it's hard to comprehend just how completely awesome the experience is. As they say, it's totally gnarly, bro.

The remote Bugaboo Mountains, in eastern British Columbia, are known for their mighty granite spires and alpine glaciers. The Bugaboos are also where heli-skiing started, back in 1965, when the world's first heli-ski lodge was built. Today, the forty-four-room Bugaboos Lodge is still the area's premier resort; if you want to heli-ski in the Bugaboos, you are staying here.

Fortunately, the remote lodge has all the bells and whistles of a luxury ski resort. Rooftop hot tub? Check. Roaring fireplaces, top-notch food, and in-room massage service? Yup. There's even a four-story climbing wall for days when the weather isn't cooperating and the helicopter is temporarily grounded.

The Basics

Bugaboos Lodge, roughly 200 miles west of Calgary, is the base for heli-skiing in the Bugaboo mountains. Transportation is by bus from Calgary to Golden, and then by helicopter from Golden to the lodge.

Heli-skiing is recommended for strong intermediate and advanced skiers. Snowboarders need to be strong (and pretty fearless) riders.

While the cost is significant, all-inclusive heli-skiing trips are comparable to high-end ski resorts (minus their crowded slopes). Expect to pay $1,000 per day including food, lodging, and lodge transfers.

THINGS TO KNOW

- × Hans Gmoser single-handedly popularized heli-skiing. Gmoser moved from Austria to Canada in the 1950s and started the first backcountry ski-outfitter in the Canadian Rockies. In 1965, a professional ski racer asked Gmoser to guide him into the remote Bugaboos. Gmoser suggested a trip by helicopter, inspired by reports of the first sightseeing trips by helicopter in the Swiss Alps. The rest is skiing history.

- × Heli-skiing has a built-in maximum when it comes to crowds. Helicopters can seat no more than ten passengers. Which means a resort like Bugaboos Lodge serves no more than seven thousand skiers per year. Compare that to the 1.5 million annual skiers who visit a typical major resort.

- × How do you make an unforgettable heli-skiing experience even *more* unforgettable? Arrive in style on the glass-domed train cars of the Rocky Mountaineer. The famous sightseeing train travels the Canadian Rockies between Vancouver and Kamloops, Lake Louise, and Banff, where you can transfer to nearby Calgary.

TRUE OR FALSE? The world's largest rodeo happens in Calgary.

True. The Calgary Stampede is a ten-day rodeo held annually in July. The event draws more than a million people and temporarily doubles the population of Calgary. Yee-haw.

RUN THE SALMON RIVER'S MIDDLE FORK

WHAT One hundred miles, three hundred rapids
WHERE Stanley, Idaho
BRAG FACTOR Low
LIKELIHOOD TO DIE Low
BEST TIME TO GO June–August
PHYSICAL DIFFICULTY Medium
COST $$$

The Middle Fork of the Salmon River is legendary. This 104-mile stretch of river flows freely through high-country forest, canyons, and bluffs in central Idaho. It also flows through the largest wilderness area in the continental United States, the 2.5-million acre Frank Church–River of No Return Wilderness.

More to the point, it's 100 miles of flat-out, straight-up white-water. You don't come to the Salmon River's Middle Fork unless you're ready to be pummeled and sprayed and splashed by raging rapids. The Middle Fork drops more than 3,000 feet over its 100-mile course, with more than three hundred (!) named rapids, each one rated at least Class III+. Many are Class IV. Aptly named Dagger Falls is Class V. This river is not for the fainthearted.

Nevertheless, don't be scared off. Numerous rafting companies guide people of all ages and experience levels down the Middle Fork. Their safety record is excellent. The more adventurous tackle the river in kayaks. Either way, once you're on the river it's incredibly special. Every evening, rafters and kayakers pull out for the night, then camp in mountain meadows, hike to a waterfall, soak in a natural hot spring, or just relax by a campfire under the stars. Not a single road mars the river's beauty. It is wild and scenic in the truest sense.

The Basics

Most river trips start in Stanley and end in Salmon River, Idaho. Your biggest decisions are how to tackle the river—paddle raft (everybody paddles), oar rig (guide paddles, everybody else hangs on), or kayak—and how many nights you want to stay on the river.

There's no right or wrong answer for the latter; it depends on how many rapids you plan to cover per day and how leisurely you want your pace to be. End-to-end trips covering the full length of the Middle Fork last five or six nights. Expect to pay $1,800 and up per person for transfers, food, lodging, and river guiding (raft or kayak).

The river's peak flow is late May to late June, the time for maximum adventure. In July and August, the weather is warmer and the river flow is more suitable for kids.

THINGS TO KNOW

- More than 100 miles of Idaho's Middle Fork River are considered "wild," the US government's highest level of protection against development and encroachment by roads. Wild rivers represent vestiges of America's native and primitive landscapes.

- The Salmon River was originally known as Lewis's River, after explorer Meriwether Lewis (of Lewis and Clark fame). It was too rough for the explorers to cross or navigate.

- Each year, thousands of salmon make the 1,800-mile run from the Pacific to spawning grounds along the Salmon River. It is one of the longest spawning runs in the world.

TRUE OR FALSE? It is illegal to chase fish in Idaho.

True. It is against the law to chase fish up or down a river in Idaho, in any manner.

HOW TO ESCAPE FAST-MOVING WATER

BASIC

Don't be arrogant; start with a "safety first" attitude. Just because you can swim does not mean you cannot drown.

Wear a life jacket, always, even if you don't want to. Pull the straps tight and never loosen them.

If you fall in, ride the current on your back, head pointing upstream, feet pointing downstream. Keep your toes just above the water's surface.

Watch for obstacles. Use your legs or feet to push off rocks and logs. The most common way to drown in rapids is being caught in, or entrapped by, an obstacle.

Do not attempt to stand up. It's dangerous to drop your feet, and there's no chance your body can resist the water's force.

ADVANCED

Be on the lookout for calmer areas, especially around river bends. When you see one, roll onto your stomach and swim downstream at a forty-five-degree angle. Do not swim straight toward shore.

In deeper rapids, instead of floating on your back, float downstream on your stomach. Maintain an angle that keeps you close to shore and avoid obstacles.

Whether swimming on your back or belly, keep yourself horizontal to the river's surface. This reduces the chances of being sucked under by a current or rapid.

Time your breathing. Inhale when you surface in the trough of a wave, and hold your breath or exhale as you ride the next whitecap. A massive gulp of water is the last thing you need.

Don't panic if you are pulled under for a long period of time. It happens. Protect your head and neck with your hands, hold your breath, and wait for the current to pull you back to the surface.

HANG WITH HIPPOS

WHAT They're cute, but deadly
WHERE Queen Elizabeth National Park, Uganda
BRAG FACTOR Medium
LIKELIHOOD TO DIE Low
BEST TIME TO GO January–February and June–July
PHYSICAL DIFFICULTY Low
COST $

It's easy to see why Queen Elizabeth National Park is Uganda's most popular wildlife destination. The huge park is famous for its diverse ecosystems: grassy savannahs to jungle forest, volcano-crater lakes to sprawling wetlands. You'll find all the usual suspects roaming the landscape, too: lion, elephant, cheetah, and leopard, plus ten primate species and more than six hundred species of birds.

The park is also famous for hippos. Kazinga Channel, a natural waterway running for 20 miles between Lake George and Lake Edward, is home to more hippos than any other place on Earth. The water teems with hippos (and with hungry Nile crocodiles!). You'll see hundreds and hundreds of hippos on a boat trip down the channel. It's considered a highlight of any visit to Queen Elizabeth National Park.

Hippos are semiaquatic and spend much of their time in the water avoiding the sun (they have no sweat glands and rely on the water to stay cool). After a day of bathing, hippos leave the water at dusk and spend the night grazing. They travel up to 5 miles and chomp more than 150 pounds of grass each night. It's why the shoreline around Kazinga Channel and lakes George and Edward are stripped bare of grasses.

Interestingly enough, hippos do not swim. They cannot. Instead hippos bounce on the bottom of lakes and rivers. On land they are surprisingly fast and can outrun humans over short distances. You have been warned: Never attempt to outrun a hippo.

The Basics

The national park organizes boat cruises up to four times a day along the Kazinga Channel. Forty-person boats depart from the Mweya Peninsula; every safari operator and lodge can organize tickets and transport. The three-hour boat ride costs less than $40.

The park is open year-round. Wildlife viewing is best during the two dry seasons from January through February and June through July.

THINGS TO KNOW

- The mighty hippopotamus, derived from the Greek word for "river horse," is the second-largest land animal in the world (only the elephant is larger). They are also among the heaviest, with adult male hippos topping six thousand pounds.

- Hippos aren't horses at all. They are most closely related to whales and porpoises.

- While hippo meat is illegal, it's considered a delicacy and sells fast when it shows up in local markets. This has led to serious conservation issues in neighboring Congo, where former militiamen use rocket launchers and dynamite to bring down hippos. A single animal can fetch up to $3,000 locally.

- In 2005, large numbers of hippos were killed in the Kazinga Channel as a result of an anthrax outbreak. The population has since recovered.

TRUE OR FALSE? Hippos kill more humans each year than any other animal in Africa.

True (if you exclude mosquitoes). Hippos are highly territorial and will charge when threatened. Most confrontations happen at night, when an unwitting villager or fisherman accidentally stumbles across the path of a hippo.

FOLLOW THE WILDEBEEST MIGRATION

WHAT The largest movement of mammals on Planet Earth
WHERE Arusha, Tanzania
BRAG FACTOR Medium
LIKELIHOOD TO DIE Low
PHYSICAL DIFFICULTY Medium
BEST TIME TO GO Year-Round
COST $$–$$$$

In Tanzania and Kenya, in eastern Africa, the countryside is wild, untouched. Look in any direction and you'll see an endless stretch of plains and rolling hills and acacia trees.

Amidst these plains, there are the animals. Immense wildebeest. Thomson's gazelles. Zebra. Lions. Cheetahs. Leopards. Hyenas. Giraffes. Hippos. Jackals. Crocodiles.

It's impossible to spend time in east Africa during the annual migration, when more than two million animals migrate between Tanzania and Kenya, and not be touched by the spectacle of life and death on the plains. It's predator and prey locked in the endless cycle of survival.

In truth, there is no single migration. The wildebeest simply trace a 500-mile circle between Serengeti National Park in Tanzania and the Maasai Mara National Reserve in Kenya on a never-ending search for food and water. The animals follow the seasonal rains over grassy savannas, through open woodlands, and across crocodile-infested rivers. There's no other spectacle like it on Earth.

The Basics

If the annual migration has a beginning, it's the mass birthing of wildebeests in January and February around Olduvai Gorge and the northern slopes of Ngorongoro Crater (a must-see site itself). Nearly four hundred thousand wildebeest calves are "dropped," or born, within a few weeks of one another.

The mass birthing is a feeding frenzy for large carnivores; lions, hyenas, and vultures are everywhere, chomping on the bones and carcasses of wildebeest calves. (On the plus side, the near-synchronous birthing overwhelms the predators' appetites and means the vast majority of wildebeest calves survive.)

In March through May, the herd moves northwest into Serengeti National Park during a short rainy season. From there, usually in May or June, the herd moves northeast toward Kenya's Maasai Mara National Reserve. It's one of the most perilous legs of the journey as it crosses many rivers filled with deadly Nile crocodiles.

From July through October, the herd settles down in the Maasai Mara. It then begins drifting south in November and December, following the rains, in the run-up to the annual birthing that marks the next loop in the endless life-and-death migration cycle.

Arusha is the self-declared "Adventure Capital" of Tanzania and a good base for organizing safaris along the southern and western loops of the annual migration. Safaris come in all shapes and varieties: small-group, private, camping rough, sleeping in basic cabins, sleeping in deluxe eco-lodges, etc. You'll travel bumpy roads in battered 4x4s, stopping frequently to take photos.

First-timers may feel more comfortable staying in safari lodges. However, tented camps bring you closer to the wild. Wherever you stay, your safari should follow the herd. Don't stay in one place. A professional driver-guide is also important. Costs range from $75 per day for basic group safaris to upwards of $800 or more.

THINGS TO KNOW

- ✕ Ngorongoro Crater and Serengeti National Park were among the first World Heritage Sites recognized in Africa by the United Nations. Together they are home to the continent's largest population of lions (more than 3,500) and to healthy, highly visible populations of cheetahs and leopards.

- ✕ A newborn wildebeest is perhaps the most coordinated juvenile mammal on the planet. Calves are usually standing two to three minutes after birth and able to outrun a lion within five minutes.

- ✕ It's common for massive herds of zebra to travel just ahead of the great wildebeest mass. Zebra and wildebeest each eat different parts of the same grass. Zebra consume the stalks; wildebeest munch on the remaining tufts.

- ✕ Besides animals, southern Tanzania is famous for fossils. In the 1950s, paleoanthropologists Mary and Louis Leakey made some of their most important discoveries (the prehuman remains of *Australopithecus boisei* and *Homo habilis*) at Olduvai Gorge and showed that humans evolved in Africa.

Who wrote most of the music for the 1994 musical *The Lion King*?

Elton John. Extra credit if you know The Lion King is the third-longest-running show on Broadway, ever.

MEET A MOB OF MEERKATS

WHAT Meerkats come in clans, mobs, and gangs—and they're all
ridiculously cute

WHERE Makgadikgadi Pans National Park, Botswana

BRAG FACTOR Medium

LIKELIHOOD TO DIE Low

BEST TIME TO GO June–July

PHYSICAL DIFFICULTY Low

COST $$$–$$$$

Botswana is home to legendary landscapes like the Kalahari Desert
and the vast Okavango Delta, the world's largest inland delta.

More than forty percent of this Texas-size country is set aside
in national parks and game reserves, teeming with animals and
birds and relatively untouched by human activity. If you're looking
for a safari experience that's thick with wildlife where you can drive
around and not encounter many other humans, Botswana is your
new favorite destination in southern Africa.

Besides elephants and hippos and the usual African big game,
Botswana is home to the continent's largest wild meerkat popu-
lation. Their habitat extends across the Kalahari Desert and into
Botswana's arid Makgadikgadi Pan, one of the world's largest salt
flats and, by far, the best location in Botswana to see meerkats in
the wild.

Meerkats are exceptionally good diggers, tunneling burrows
that can extend dozens of feet underground. Meerkats are highly
sociable—they live in mobs, or small groups, of up to forty or fifty
individuals. They are also excellent hunters, with insanely sensi-
tive hearing and eyesight. Similar to wolf packs, meerkats hunt as
a group, outsmarting the unlucky scorpion, beetle, or lizard that
crosses their path.

When the colony is hunting, meerkats take turns standing guard, surveying the horizon for predators and vocalizing and communicating with the colony nonstop. When a predator such as an eagle, snake, or jackal is spotted, the meerkat sentinel lets out a distinctive bark and the entire colony scampers underground to safety.

Meeting meerkats up close is the experience you're after. Meerkats are charismatic creatures. Imagine the most playful puppy and cutest kitten you've ever seen; now smush them together and, voila!—you have the meerkat. Fortunately, meerkats are not frightened by humans and are relatively easy to observe and photograph. Kids love the experience.

The Basics

Wild meerkats are shy and vigilant, and can be frustrating to view. Your best option is a meerkat safari in the Makgadikgadi Pan between May and July. This is peak season for viewing meerkats in the wild.

Colonies of human-habituated meerkats are active year-round and accessed in the Makgadikgadi Pan area out of Jack's Camp, Camp Kalahari, San Camp, and Planet Baobab. There's the added benefit of witnessing Africa's second-largest migration if you visit between January and March; during this short, intense wet season, the grassy plains north of the Makgadikgadi Pan swell with zebra and wildebeest.

Botswana safaris are generally on the expensive side; expect to pay $700 to $900 per person, per day, for all-inclusive safaris departing from Botswana's capital, Gaborone.

THINGS TO KNOW

- ✗ Botswana is an unlikely success story. It was poor and sparsely populated when it achieved independence from Britain in 1966. The discovery of diamond deposits the following year could have been a disaster for the country. Instead, Botswana's first president, Sir Seretse Khama, instituted civilian leadership unmarred by corruption and built a well-managed national park system. Botswana today is one Africa's most stable and prosperous countries.

- ✗ The Kalahari Meerkat Project, a scientific research center in neighboring South Africa, has successfully habituated wild meerkat colonies to humans. Similar efforts are underway in Botswana.

- ✗ Meerkats are immune to most snake venom. Scientists are studying how meerkats do it, hoping it's possible to make a human vaccine against snake venom to protect the thirty thousand people who die each year in sub-Saharan Africa from snake bites.

TRUE OR FALSE? Meerkats sleep in on rainy days.

True. Much like humans, meerkats don't like to get out of bed when it's raining.

GET LOST IN A BLIZZARD OF BATS

WHAT Just you in the treetops with ten million fruit bats
WHERE Kasanka National Park, Zambia
BRAG FACTOR High (few people know about it)
LIKELIHOOD TO DIE Low (these are not vampire bats)
BEST TIME TO GO Mid-October–early December
PHYSICAL DIFFICULTY Low
COST $$$–$$$$

It's one of the world's best-kept wildlife secrets. Each year in late October, the world's largest mammalian migration happens in the evergreen swamps of Zambia's Kasanka National Park, near the border with the Democratic Republic of the Congo.

It lasts just a few short weeks. More than ten million African fruit bats gather, vast swirling columns that stretch for thousands of feet in every direction. Each evening at dusk, they pour out of the forest, wave after wave, dense swarms off to feed on fruit and mangos in Zambia's lush forests. The millions of chirping bats return from feasting in the early morning hours as the sun rises, to the same five-acre mahogany and milkwood forest. They roost upside down in the dense tree canopy, jostling and nudging for position on every branch and trunk.

The experience is over quickly. Once the bats settle in for the day, there is not much to do but wait for the return flight of ten million bats to the feeding grounds at dusk.

Kasanka is Zambia's only privately managed national park, and is also one of its smallest parks. It's not the best safari destination in Zambia, though there are plenty of elephants and big game to occupy a few pleasant days. The real draw is the birdlife—Kasanka is one of Africa's premier birding destinations—and, of course, the bats.

The Basics

Bat season runs for roughly ninety days from October through December, with peak viewing in late October and early November.

You can view bats from anywhere within the park. The best viewing spots are the treetop hides, 70 feet up in the canopy and at eye level with the bats.

Unless you're a serious birder, most visitors combine a two-day visit to Kasanka during bat season with a few nights at one of Zambia's better-known safari parks, such as Kafue and South Luangwa.

THINGS TO KNOW

* African fruit bats are known as flying foxes. And rightly so. The have bright orange eyes, are the size of small puppies, and have wingspans approaching 3 feet in length. If they ate anything other than fruit, say, the blood of humans, they'd be scary as hell.

* For most of the year, the bats live in the neighboring Democratic Republic of the Congo. They arrive in Zambia just as the trees bear fruit: mango, waterberries, wild loquat, and red milkwood berries. Each bat consumes up to five pounds of fruit per night. By the end of the migration, most fruit trees within a fifteen-mile radius are stripped bare.

* Bats play a critical role in the health of forests. They spread the seeds of many trees through their feces.

* Bats at Kasanka are generally safe from predators. Their biggest concerns are large raptors hunting them at dusk and dawn, and crocodiles. The roosting bats are so heavy that drooping branches often break away from trees and fall into the river, providing the perfect snack for a hungry crocodile.

TRUE OR FALSE? There are no blood-sucking vampire bats in Africa.

True. The only three species of vampire bats are all native to Central and South America.

OVERNIGHT WITH EMPEROR PENGUINS

WHAT Yes, you really can camp overnight in the Antarctic
WHERE Weddell Sea, Antarctica
BRAG FACTOR High
LIKELIHOOD TO DIE Medium (helicopters in Antarctica—what could go wrong?!)
BEST TIME TO GO November–January
PHYSICAL DIFFICULTY Medium
COST $$$$–$$$$$

The remote Antarctic Peninsula is home to the nutrient-rich waters of the Weddell Sea. It's a stunningly beautiful setting. The sea is framed by 1,200 miles of glacier-bound mountains, massive ice shelves and towering glacial cliffs. A deep-ocean upwelling of nutrient-rich water feeds the sea, offering sustenance for any creature that can handle the cold.

And it is cold. Bone-chillingly cold. Average daytime temperatures range from 10 degrees Fahrenheit to 25 degrees Fahrenheit, plunging to -20 degrees when the wind picks up or a storm blows through.

Unless you're an Antarctic scientist, there's only one reason to put up with the extreme conditions. It's a chance to visit—and possibly camp alongside (if the weather cooperates and you don't balk at the cost)—an emperor penguin colony.

Each winter (which starts in March in Antarctica), emperor penguins travel more than 50 miles across the ice to their breeding grounds. Males arrive first, positioning themselves on the ice to attract female mating partners with flashy displays and courtship calls.

Starting in May or June, females leave the breeding grounds to feed in the ocean, leaving males to incubate the eggs. Over the next few months, the males must keep their eggs safe and warm, and ensure their own survival, in some of the coldest and most difficult conditions on Earth—and on empty stomachs! Males do not eat for more than two months while waiting for the chicks to hatch.

To fend off the cold, males huddle together in groups, taking turns moving to the inside of the circle where it's warmer. Eggs are balanced on their feet, kept warm inside a layer of feathered skin.

Finally the females return, regurgitating food for the hatchlings to eat. It's now the females' turn to care for the young penguins. Males head off to sea for a hard-earned meal of krill and fish.

The Basics

A handful of operators visit the Emperor penguin rookery on Snow Hill Island, which faces the Weddell Sea on the eastern side of the Antarctic Peninsula.

It's closer to South America than any other part of Antarctica. Round-trip cruises depart from Ushuaia in Argentina. The typical cruise itinerary is ten to fourteen days and includes ship-to-shore helicopter flights, landing within a short walk of the Snow Hill Island penguin colony. It's a slow process: Ships carry up to one hundred passengers, and most helicopters accommodate six people per flight. On the ground you'll have an hour to visit with the penguins before returning to the ship by helicopter. Expect to pay $10,000 per person, depending on the level of comfort you crave.

Alternatively, air-only (no boats, no seasickness!) tours depart from Punta Arenas, Chile. These fly overnight to Antarctica's Union Glacier, then fly to the Emperor penguin colony at Gould Bay for two to four nights of tent camping on the ice. It's one of the world's most remote campsites and the only Antarctic tourist camping on sea ice.

Tents are set up within a mile or so of the colony, far enough not to disturb but close enough to allow multiple visits. This is high-end camping and you'll pay for the privilege of sleeping in Antarctica within earshot of Emperor penguins: a whopping $40,000 to $50,000 per person. Super-size your experience with a fly-over of latitude 90 degrees south—the geographic South Pole—for an extra $10,000. No, this is not cheap.

All trips happen in a relatively short window: between November and early January, before the Antarctic winters sets in.

THINGS TO KNOW

- ✕ Emperor penguins are the largest of the seventeen known species of penguin. They are nearly 4 feet tall and weigh up to sixty-five pounds.

- ✕ Only a third of Emperor penguin chicks survive their first year. Most are eaten by seabirds or die from hunger. Fortunately, the overall Emperor penguin population of six hundred thousand is stable.

- ✕ Emperor penguins are excellent swimmers. They can stay submerged for twenty minutes and dive to depths of nearly 2,000 feet. Their main waterborne predators are leopard seals and killer whales.

What do film stars Elijah Wood, Robin Williams, Hugh Jackman, Nicole Kidman, and Hugo Weaving have in common?

They all starred as Emperor penguins in the 2006 animated musical Happy Feet. If you prefer penguin documentaries to musicals, check out March of the Penguins (2005) or David Attenborough's Frozen Planet (2011).

TREK BY HORSE IN ICELAND

WHAT Glaciers and geysers on horseback
WHERE Húsavík and Kálfhóll, Iceland
BRAG FACTOR Medium
LIKELIHOOD TO DIE Low
BEST TIME TO GO July–August
PHYSICAL DIFFICULTY Medium
COST $$$–$$$$

There are many ways to explore Iceland. One of the best—and least known—is by horse.

Iceland itself is surreal. Boiling geysers shoot water into the sky. Crashing waterfalls, frigid glaciers, bubbling hot springs, ice-filled lagoons, barren moonlike landscapes paired with lush golden vegetation. At times it seems otherworldly, as if you've somehow magically arrived on a distant moon circling Jupiter or Saturn. Iceland feels like no place on Earth.

The horse tracks in the north of Iceland are frequently ranked among the world's best by travel magazines. Between Húsavík and Lake Mývatn, trails weave among the volcanic features and strange rock formations, through Ásbyrgi Canyon and into Vatnajökull National Park and past Dettifoss, Europe's largest waterfall. You'll see the rocks at Hljóðaklettar and the photogenic glacier-encrusted cone of Snæfellsjökull volcano.

In southern Iceland, the Golden Circle trail covers the three key attractions on this classic route: the hot springs of Geysir, the mighty Gullfoss Waterfall (Iceland's most visited landmark), and Thingvellir National Park, which happens to be a UNESCO World Heritage Site.

And you'll see it all on horseback. Some treks require extensive riding experience; others are open to families and riders of all levels.

The days are long, up to five or six hours of riding, so all you really need is stamina. And an appetite for lamb and fish, Iceland's staple trail foods.

You'll also need to adjust to the Icelandic horse. Unique among all horses, it has five natural gaits: the walk, trot, and canter familiar to most riders, plus the *tölt* and the flying pace. The tölt, a smooth four-beat gait with one foot always touching the ground, allows the rider an almost bounce-free ride. The flying pace is a fast, high-speed gait, used for short distances and in racing.

Icelandic horses have these gaits naturally, and you'll spend the first day of any ride getting accustomed to it.

The Basics

The highlands of northern Iceland are best for experienced riders. Treks start at Bjarnastaðir Farm near Húsavík and head out into the area around Lake Mývatn. Itineraries usually include five or six days of riding, with accommodation in rustic mountain cabins, plus airfare from Reykjavík to Húsavík in northern Iceland. Expect to pay $1,600 or more per person.

Many of the southern horse treks, including the Golden Circle tour, are open to intermediate riders. It's an easy bus transfer from Reykjavík to the Kálfhóll horse farm, where riders gather before heading to Gullfoss Waterfall and the hot springs of Geysir. Itineraries range two to six days.

Iceland's main riding season is short. The earliest rides depart in June and finish in late August or early September.

Two-night northern lights treks from Reykjavík (riding by day, admiring the aurora borealis at night next to a toasty campfire) are offered for intermediate riders in October and November, and again in March and April.

THINGS TO KNOW

- Don't call them ponies. Iceland's horses are small, but they are *not* ponies.

- Icelandic horses come in more than forty different color combinations, with more than a hundred variations. Icelandic may not have fifty words for snow, but they do have specific words for at least one hundred of the most common horse colors and patterns: *bleikálóttur*, *litförótt*, *móvindóttur*, *svartur*, *rauðjarpur*, *dökkjarpur* . . . you get the idea.

- Vikings first brought horses to Iceland in the ninth century. No horse has been introduced since, so Iceland's horses have had more than a thousand years to develop their unique gaits and traits. Horses that leave Iceland are not allowed to return.

- *Reiðskóli*, or outdoor riding schools, give novice riders a chance to improve their horsemanship and master the Icelandic horse's five gaits. Five-day programs cost less than $200. Kids love it.

Which of the following is not a traditional Icelandic food: *hákarl*, "fermented ice shark," raw horse meat, Puffin heart (served warm), pickled ram's testicles, or seal flippers?

Trick question. They are all traditional Icelandic foods. Bon appétit!

DOGSLED WITH THE INUIT

WHAT Mush!
WHERE Kulusuk, Greenland
BRAG FACTOR High (who do *you* know who's visited Greenland?!)
LIKELIHOOD TO DIE Low
BEST TIME TO GO February–April
PHYSICAL DIFFICULTY High
COST $$$$

The Inuit, the indigenous peoples of the Arctic, have lived and worked together with dogs for more than four thousand years, proving that dogs may be man's best friend the world over. For the Inuit, dogs provide the ability to survive the harsh polar environment. Dogs pull *qamutiik,* "native ice sleds." They are hunting partners, used to track caribou and seals on the sea ice, and they guard remote hunting camps against nighttime predation from polar bears and wolves.

There's no better place than Greenland to experience this deep, almost spiritual, connection between human and dog. The majority of Greenland's residents are Inuit and Inuit culture remains strong on the island. In winter and spring, it's even possible to dogsled with traditional Inuit hunters, exploring the wild and frozen landscapes of eastern Greenland, known as Tunu in Greenlandic.

Dogsledding remains an essential part of life in the Inuit community of Kulusuk. Tours can be as simple as a day trip or a journey of several days deep into the Arctic wilderness, sleeping in huts on the sea ice, and hunting along the way to provide food for the dog team.

The scenery is out of this world: frozen fjords choked with icebergs, massive glaciers, towering mountains, and occasional displays of the haunting aurora borealis. The wilderness area spans more than 1,500 miles and is home to fewer than four thousand people. Over five or six days you visit some of the most far removed communities in the most remote region of Greenland, all by dogsled.

You'll bag a seal on the way if you are really lucky. Raw seal meat is delicious.

The Basics

It takes years of experience to drive a dog team alone. However with just a little training, you are allowed to brake, assist in navigation, and look after the dogs. Most of the time you'll simply sit back and relax on the sled, keeping an eye out for wildlife. Most dogsled treks are organized to maximize wildlife viewing.

While most normal people don't contemplate a visit to the Arctic in winter, it's actually the best time of year for dogsledding. From February to April, the snow is dense and the ice is thick, making it possible to travel the entire length of Greenland by dogsled. Summer dogsledding is only possible if the snow and ice pack from the previous winter are exceptionally good.

The Inuit village of Kulusuk, home to 250 hearty souls, is a collection of wooden cabins set on a frozen bay. A small airstrip handles flights to and from Reykjavik, Iceland, and from Greenland's main international airport at Kangerlussuaq. Counterintuitively, the flight from Reykjavik is much shorter.

There's no such thing as an independent dogsled tour in eastern Greenland. You'll need to prebook an organized tour. These run from four to ten days, and include dog sledding, food, accommodations, and round-trip flights to Kulusuk from Iceland or Sweden. You'll pay between $4,000 and $8,000.

THINGS TO KNOW

- Dogsledding is culturally important to the Inuit. It's also safer than snowmobiling, which is used increasingly more often for short-duration hunting trips. An experienced dog team can find and stay on a trail in the worst weather conditions.

- The world's largest dogsled race is Norway's Femundløpet, held in February in the town of Røros. Alaska's famous Iditarod dogsled race is held annually in March.

- Greenland is a newly trendy adventure-sport destination. Even so, tourism to Greenland is still in its infancy. In the record-breaking year of 2016, fewer than ninety-seven thousand people visited.

- One of Greenland's newest attractions is the majestic Ilulissat Icefjord, declared a UNESCO World Heritage Site in 2004.

TRUE OR FALSE? The US Postal Service regularly delivers mail in Alaska by dogsled.

False. However, it was true until 1963, when regular dogsled service ended.

HOW TO BUILD
A SNOW SHELTER

BASIC

A tall tree is the simplest and most convenient snow shelter. Use the natural hollow in the snow around the trunk as the basis for a shelter. Pile up snow on all sides to protect against weather. Cut low branches on the side away from your shelter as bedding. If you light a fire, do it away from your shelter to avoid melting snow in your shelter area.

Look for rock formations with natural notches or openings. You need only enough covered space to fit your body when lying flat. Line the ground with branches or vegetation, and pile up snow at least 3 feet high to create a barrier against weather.

Build a snow trench if there are no trees or natural cover. Dig a trench perpendicular to the wind, 1 foot deep and slightly longer and wider than your body. Line it with branches, vegetation, or a tarp. Use a shovel to pound snow into 2-by-3-foot blocks, creating an A-frame style enclosure above the trench. Use another ice block to close off one end of

the trench. Cover the opposite end loosely with branches or a poncho. Your body heat will warm the inside of the trench by ten to twenty degrees.

ADVANCED

Build a snow cave. It's possible in snow that's at least 6 feet deep (otherwise collapse is a risk). Dig into an existing snowdrift or pile up snow yourself, making a compact mound as large as possible. Dig out an arched, vertical entranceway (on the downhill side, if relevant) roughly 2 feet wide, 3 feet tall, and 2 feet deep. Next, create a T shape by digging out a rectangular section above the entrance, to an equal depth of 2 feet. Continue digging out the horizontal sleeping area for another 3 or 4 feet, making sure the ceiling is rounded. Dig a hole at least 6 inches in diameter at the top to allow carbon dioxide to escape. Finally, compact snow into ice and block the horizontal space. Climb in and up into the elevated sleeping area, which traps heat and allows cold air to flow down and out.

Build an igloo. Start on a downhill slope to save effort. Outline the outer wall in snow (no more than 8 feet in diameter) and pack down the snow inside the circle. Use the snow inside the wall's perimeter to shape or cut brick-shaped mounds of snow, roughly 3 feet long, 1 foot high, and 6 inches thick. Build from the inside out, laying one row of snow blocks at a time, and angling the lowest layers so the walls slope inward. Eventually the blocks will join at the top. Cut a door only after finishing the dome from the inside.

Don't let your door or trench face into the wind. In the immortal words of Homer Simpson, "D'oh!" Always position the entrance perpendicular to the wind.

RIDE A CAMEL WITH BEDOUINS

WHAT Lawrence of Arabia for the Twenty-first Century
WHERE Wadi Rum, Jordan
BRAG FACTOR Medium
LIKELIHOOD TO DIE Low
BEST TIME TO GO March–May, September–October
PHYSICAL DIFFICULTY Moderate
COST $$

While not quite a noble beast—all camels bite and spit, and some are downright ornery—the single-humped Arabian camel is deeply associated with the Bedouin. There was a time when tribes of nomadic Bedouin crossed the vast deserts of Iraq, Syria, Palestine, and Jordan on the back of Arabian camels.

Nowadays, the Bedouin have exchanged camels for pickup trucks (pickups don't bite). The camel is still used as a beast of burden, and definitely for its meat and milk. Camels are also good for business; Bedouins in Jordan, for example, near the tourist sites of Petra and Wadi Rum, maintain small camel herds and take visitors on overnight treks deep into the desert, through some of the country's most starkly beautiful terrain.

Shuffling through the desert on a camel, sleeping under the stars in Bedouin camps, listening to traditional music by a campfire . . . it's not quite living like Lawrence of Arabia, but it's an incredible experience and worth every bite and grunt that a cantankerous camel may send your way.

Wadi Rum, Jordan's largest *wadi* (dry river valley) is the best place to begin a camel trek. Wadi Rum itself is one of Jordan's top attractions, a unique landscape of shifting sand dunes surrounded by *jebel* (mountains) and a network of canyons with cliffs towering hundreds of feet above the valley floor.

The Basics

Most people visit Wadi Rum in a noisy, bumpy 4x4 and don't get to experience the overwhelming silence of the desert. On a camel, as you trek deeper into the desert, you'll see fewer and fewer vehicles until you eventually have the magnificent desert all to yourself.

Camel treks from Wadi Rum last anywhere from a few hours (not worth it) to overnight. There are also multiday treks all the way to Petra (seven days) or Aqaba (five days).

If you're in doubt, consider a two- or three-day trek within the confines of Wadi Rum. Be sure your itinerary includes the ancient Nabatean inscriptions at Jebel Khazali; Lawrence's Spring, a freshwater pool tucked inside a canyon at the foot of Jebel Rum, and made famous by T. E. Lawrence; and the ridiculously photogenic rock bridges of Um Fruth and Burdah.

Tours typically include all food and lodging. No special equipment or training is required. Bedouin camps are typically a dozen or so tents sleeping two or three people, with plenty of warm blankets (winter nights are chilly) and generous Bedouin hospitality. Expect to pay $100 to $200 per night, per person.

Camel treks are offered year-round, though weather-wise, the best times to visit Wadi Rum are spring (March to May) and autumn (September to October).

THINGS TO KNOW

- × Aside from its beauty, Wadi Rum is famous for being the central setting of *Seven Pillars of Wisdom*, T. E. Lawrence's account of his involvement in the Arab Revolt of 1916.

- × Many scenes from the hugely popular 1962 film *Lawrence of Arabia* were shot on location at Wadi Rum.

- × There are no wild camels left in Jordan. The last died out in the eighteenth century. Any camels you see today belong to someone.

- Besides transporting tourists, Wadi Rum camels are bred to be racing camels. The sport is a big deal in Saudi Arabia. Saudi scouts pay local Bedouin camel breeders top dollar for a good prospect.

TRUE OR FALSE? The former king of Jordan met his wife on the set of the film *Lawrence of Arabia*.

True. Jordan's King Hussein not only allowed his army to appear as extras in the movie, he also met Antoinette Gardiner, a British film assistant, while touring the set. They married in 1962 and their son, Abdullah II, ascended to the throne in 1999.

TRAVEL THE ANCIENT SILK ROAD

WHAT Seven thousand miles, six countries, eight time zones
WHERE Beijing to Istanbul
BRAG FACTOR High
LIKELIHOOD TO DIE Low
BEST TIME TO GO May–September
PHYSICAL DIFFICULTY Medium
COST $$–$$$$

The Silk Road. The name evokes adventure and a time when merchants traveled between legendary trading hubs such as Kashgar and Samarkand in vast caravans of horses and camels. The trade route connected China and central Asia with Europe, following the northern borders of China, India, Persia, and Arabia, and ending in the Levant (modern Syria, Lebanon, and Turkey) on the Mediterranean Sea.

From the west came cotton, ivory, wool, and gold; from the east came tea, jade, spices, gunpowder, and, of course, silk. In both directions flowed culture, religion, new inventions, and commerce. It's no understatement to say the Silk Road was the most important long-distance communication network in all of history for people and ideas to spread across the settled world.

There has never been a single Silk Road. Instead, it's a network of interconnected routes with two main branches extending west from China's ancient commercial centers: a northern route skirting the Taklamakan Desert, and a southern route through the rugged Karakoram Mountains (sections of the modern Karakoram Highway in Pakistan and China follow this ancient southern route).

The concept of the Silk Road has fascinated Europeans for more than a century; the very name *Silk Road* was coined by a German explorer in the nineteenth century, while he was attempting to uncover and map the ancient routes.

While there is no single modern route to follow, in 2014 Silk Roads: the Routes Network of the Chang'an-Tianshan Corridor was designated a UNESCO World Heritage Site. If you're looking for one route to cover end-to-end, this 3,100-mile stretch crossing China, Kazakhstan, and Kyrgyzstan is the one. It begins in Luoyang, China, the Silk Road's traditional eastern starting point, and hits Xi'an (think: terracotta army), Kashgar and its famous bazaar, the hanging temples and caves at Maijishan, and remote sections of the Great Wall.

Or you can tackle a major branch of the Silk Road in its entirety. A good choice is traveling from Beijing to Istanbul, crossing China, Kyrgyzstan, Uzbekistan, Turkmenistan, Iran, and Turkey. It's an amazing trip, more than 7,000 miles across six countries by foot, bus, minivan, taxi, train—whatever it takes. It's possible to do it solo, without assistance over three or four months, and plenty of backpackers do. Or sign up with a tour company that specializes in Silk Road itineraries. Either way, very few modern travelers can claim they've traveled the Silk Road end to end.

The Basics

Because winter can be brutal in the mountains of central Asia, May through September is the best time of year to travel the Silk Road. Nearly every Silk Road route traverses deserts—the vast Taklamakan, Gobi, and Arabian—that are scorching hot in summer. Avoid midsummer travel if possible.

Much of the Silk Road travels through majority-Muslim areas. It's important to note the dates of Ramadan (a month-long period of daytime fasting) before locking in your travel dates.

Visas are another issue for modern Silk Road travelers. Azerbaijan, China, Mongolia, Tajikistan, and Uzbekistan all require visas. Managing the paperwork can be time-consuming and frustrating. Turkmenistan requires a certified letter of invitation from either a private individual or (if you're on an organized tour) a business. Kazakhstan and Kyrgyzstan both waive visas for US citizens who stay less than thirty days.

Iran's visa situation is fluid. While it's still not possible for independent US travelers to obtain visas for travel in Iran, Americans have been allowed to visit as part of group tours booked from the United Kingdom.

Group overland tours—some as long as forty-five to fifty days—are not cheap at $10,000 or more per person. The benefits are easy logistics and hassle-free border crossings. An unexpected benefit is the slower pace and opportunity to camp in the mountains, deserts, and grasslands and meet local Uighur, Kyrgyz, Uzbek, and Turkmen living in the shadows of the ancient trade route. This is much harder to accomplish if you're traveling independently and taking buses and trains from one city to the next.

THINGS TO KNOW

- ✱ The Silk Road brought immense wealth to both China and Europe. It also brought death. In the 1340s, outbreaks of deadly bubonic plague—the Black Death—flowed east from Asia to Europe, killing as many as half of all Europeans within a decade.

- ✱ The Silk Road operated for more than fifteen centuries from 130 B.C. (when the Han dynasty officially opened to western trade) until 1453 (when the Ottoman Empire boycotted trade with Europe and closed the main routes).

- ✱ Some historians do not like the name *Silk Road*. They argue silk was a relatively unimportant commodity compared to spices and, especially, paper, which quickly replaced parchment in the west and bamboo in the east.

- ✱ The Silk Road's most famous western traveler was Marco Polo. He was a merchant from Venice who spent twenty-four years crisscrossing central Asia and China, mostly working as an ambassador to the Pope on behalf of the Mongol emperor, Kublai Khan.

TRUE OR FALSE? Marco Polo introduced the concept of paper money to Europe.

True. The Mongol empire was among the first to use paper money. Marco Polo assumed that sorcery or alchemy was involved in transforming trees into currency. But no, it was just paper and ink, a revolutionary idea to Europeans accustomed to money as metal coins minted from gold and silver.

RIDE THE ORIENT EXPRESS

WHAT A luxurious rail journey through history
WHERE Paris to Istanbul
BRAG FACTOR High
LIKELIHOOD TO DIE Low
BEST TIME TO GO August
PHYSICAL DIFFICULTY Low
COST $$$$$

Intrigue, espionage, and luxury—the original Orient Express had it all. The famous line's inaugural route, in 1883, ran from Paris to Vienna. In 1889 train service was added to Constantinople (modern Istanbul) and later to Strasbourg, Vienna, Belgrade, and Budapest. The newspapers of the day dubbed it the Orient Express even though Istanbul was as close to the "Orient" as the train would ever travel.

The resurrected Orient Express leaves just once a year, usually in mid-August. It pulls out of Paris's Gare de l'Est train station and, four days later, rolls into Turkey's capital, Istanbul, with overnight stops en route in Budapest, Hungary and Bucharest, Romania.

This is no ordinary train. You travel in pure and unfettered luxury, on meticulously restored sleeper and saloon cars from the 1920s. You have a personal steward. Your three-course lunches and four-course dinners are presented in the dining car, black-tie and evening dress preferred.

You can never be overdressed on the modern Orient Express.

The Basics

The Orient Express made its last official run from Istanbul in 1977 and disappeared from the European train timetable completely in 2007, the victim of low-cost airlines and high-speed trains. The service was resurrected—luxury and all—as the Venice-Simplon Orient Express, a private company that uses original carriages from the line's glory days in the 1920s and '30s.

You are traveling in wonderfully restored rolling stock, which means there are no private bathrooms (these didn't exist in the 1920s) and that heating is powered by a coal stove at the end of each carriage. So very quaint.

One twist of the modern service is that you do not sleep aboard the train. Instead you overnight in luxury hotels in Budapest and Bucharest. This enables city sightseeing and the chance to shower or bathe.

The cost? But a trifle. Just $20,000 for two adults. The price includes all food and lodging between Paris and Istanbul, plus sightseeing day trips from Budapest and Bucharest.

THINGS TO KNOW

- ✕ If you prefer a shorter—and less expensive—rail journey through history, the Orient Express offers an annual Istanbul to Venice itinerary, departing in September. It's $10,000 for two adults.

- ✕ The Orient Express was once the most luxurious, most comfortable, and fastest way to travel from Europe's western edge, at Calais, to its easternmost point in Istanbul.

- ✕ No Orient Express ever traveled beyond Istanbul. However, an extension in 1930 called the Taurus Express carried travelers from Istanbul into Syria, Iraq, and Palestine.

- ✕ The Orient Express gained a reputation for mystery and hijinks in the 1930s as Europe braced for World War II. The reputation was cemented by Agatha Christie's 1934 novel, *Murder on the Orient Express.*

×   The Orient Express makes other literary appearances in
    Bram Stoker's *Dracula*, Graham Greene's *Travels with My
    Aunt*, and Ian Fleming's *From Russia, with Love*.

TRUE OR FALSE? When Agatha Christie published her famous novel
Murder on the Orient Express, nobody in real life had ever been
murdered on the train.

*True. The first murder on the Orient Express did not happen until the
year after Christie's book was published.*

EXPLORE THE GALÁPAGOS ISLANDS

WHAT Like no place on Earth, above or below the water
WHERE Galápagos Islands, Ecuador
BRAG FACTOR Medium
LIKELIHOOD TO DIE Low
BEST TIME TO GO December–January, July–August
PHYSICAL DIFFICULTY Low
COST $$$

The Galápagos Islands are a bucket-list destination for anybody interested in wildlife. The archipelago, 600 miles due west of Ecuador, is a remote outpost in the middle of the Pacific Ocean, a land of lava formations and tropical beaches teeming with life. Wildlife viewing is what draws thousands of people each year to the islands. Many of the land animals lack natural predators and are unbothered by the presence of humans. They are fearless.

The archipelago's most famous visitor, Charles Darwin, began to form his theories of natural selection and evolution here, and it's easy to see why. As one of the most biologically diverse spots on the planet, the Galápagos are home to birds and animals found nowhere else: marine iguanas, giant tortoises, blue-footed boobies, frigate birds, and flightless cormorants.

Underwater is equally stunning; the islands sit at a point where seven major ocean currents come together, mingling nutrient-rich cold waters from the south and west with warmer currents from the north. This convergence nourishes many unique marine species (more than 20 percent of the Galápagos marine life is endemic) and supports the world's northernmost colony of penguins, not to mention large transitory populations of manta rays and hammerhead sharks.

The Basics

The Galápagos comprise thirteen major islands, six smaller islands, and more than one hundred islets. Each major island has its own distinctive landscape and is protected as part of the Galápagos National Park. (In fact, more than 97 percent of the Galápagos Islands are inside the national park.)

Isabela Island is the largest and hosts major attractions including the Arnaldo Tupiza Giant Tortoise Breeding Center. Santa Cruz is the most populated, with the best infrastructure. It's also home to the Charles Darwin Research Station, a worthwhile museum dedicated to Darwin and his theories. Visits to most of the islands are not allowed without a guide licensed by the national park.

It's possible to book day trips to other islands from Santa Cruz, but most people opt to explore the Galápagos by boat, typically on a six- to ten-day cruise that visits the outer, more remote islands. The national park restricts the size of boats to one hundred passengers; smaller fifteen- to thirty-passenger cruises are also available. Expect to pay roughly $2,500 for seven days on a midsize boat including park fees, guide, meals, and air transfers to and from Ecuador. Of course, you can spend significantly more (small ship, longer itinerary, VIP treatment) or significantly less (shorter cruise, large boat, a few nights on Santa Cruz Island making day trips to other islands).

About eighty thousand people visit the Galápagos each year. When you go depends on what's important to you. A hot rainy season (warmer temperatures, calmer waters) runs late December through May. A cooler dry season (heavier seas, but popular with divers thanks to the colder waters) runs June through November. The most popular (and hence busiest) times are December to January and July to August.

The only direct flights to the Galápagos Islands are from mainland Ecuador via the cities of Quito or Guayaquil.

THINGS TO KNOW

* Want to see foot-long centipedes eating rats? You can. Darwin's goliath centipede, found on many islands, is the largest centipede on Earth and will eat lizards, iguanas, and rats when it can catch them.

* Keen to dive with hammerheads and whale sharks? Darwin and Wolf islands are where the liveaboard boats go, between June and November in the dry season.

* Are you a penguin lover? Then you'll want to visit Tagus Cove on Isabela. It boasts the largest population of Galápagos penguins.

* Marine iguanas, sea lions, and flightless cormorants? Head to the volcanically active island of Fernandina.

* If you travel by boat, always ask the captain to get you ashore early, before 6:00 A.M. if possible. You want to beat the heat and the crowds.

* Days and nights in the Galápagos are equal in length (you're smack dab on the Equator). There is no daylight savings, so there's roughly twelve hours of sunshine year-round.

What was the very first World Heritage Site designated by the United Nations?

Trick question. There is no single "first" site. Twelve sites (including two in Ecuador—Quito and the Galápagos) were included on the 1978 inaugural list. The Galápagos are unique because they now have dual status; both the land and the sea around the islands are recognized separately as World Heritage Sites.

DIVE WITH GREAT WHITE SHARKS

WHAT Live every week like it's Shark Week
WHERE Cape Town, South Africa
BRAG FACTOR Medium
LIKELIHOOD TO DIE Low
PHYSICAL DIFFICULTY Low
BEST TIME TO GO May–September
COST $

For some people it's a nightmarish vision from hell: being submerged in shark-infested waters, surrounded by circling great whites, coming face to face with one of the world's true apex predators.

Cue the *Jaws*-inspired theme music . . . duh-nuh . . . duh-nuh . . .

The reality, of course, is only slightly less dramatic. Yes, you are submerged in shark-infested waters. And yes, you are surrounded by fearsome great white sharks. However, you're not thrashing about in the water. You're in a steel cage protected by thick plexiglass. It's safe enough that no diving experience is required.

There are a handful of places in the world where you can dive year-round with great white sharks. Two of the best are the South African towns of Gansbaai (two hours from Cape Town) and Mossel Bay (five hours from Cape Town). Great whites don't appear on a fixed schedule, so depending on the weather and water temperatures, dive companies sometimes depart from Seal Island or False Bay, right on the outskirts of Cape Town.

The Basics

The best time to dive with great whites is May to September, over the South African winter, when the water visibility is best and sharks are most numerous.

No experience is required. Numerous tour companies offer guided shark dives for $125–$150 per person, typically with all diving gear and safety equipment included.

THINGS TO KNOW

- ✕ The largest great white ever measured in South Africa was nearly 20 feet long and caught offshore of Gansbaai.

- ✕ Sharks of many different species are attracted to this stretch of South African coast for two reasons: cold-water upwellings and large colonies of penguins and fur seals. It's a delicious smorgasbord for predators such as sharks.

- ✕ Be warned that nearly everybody on the shark boats gets seasick, at least once. The swells are large, and the weather can be rough. Come prepared.

- ✕ Dive operators have been heavily criticized for using chum (bloody scraps of fish) to attract sharks. Besides habituating sharks to the presence of man—not to mention, associating the site of people with yummy bloody fish!—companies formerly used shark parts in the chum mix. This is now illegal to help protect the world's threatened populations of sharks.

- ✕ There has been no recorded instance of a cage diver being killed by a shark. However—and it is a major however—great whites have breached cages and attacked divers. It is extremely rare. But it has happened. . . .

TRUE OR FALSE? Great white sharks have no bones.

True. All shark skeletons are made exclusively of cartilage. And no, shark teeth don't count—they are made of dentin, which is stronger and denser than bone (the better to bite you with!).

HOW TO SURVIVE A SHARK ATTACK

BASIC

Shark bites are extremely uncommon. You're far more likely to be struck by lightning or to die from being hit in the head by a falling coconut. *However, avoid swimming or surfing in areas where the three most dangerous sharks—great white, tiger, and bull—may be present.*

Avoid areas where fishing boats congregate. Struggling fish and bloody bait are prime attractors for sharks.

Be extra cautious swimming at sunrise and sunset, or late at night. They are the most common times for shark attacks.

Avoid bleeding or urinating in the water. Sharks can detect tiny amounts of either from miles away and will swim closer to investigate. Get out of the water if you cut yourself. Menstruating women should not swim in shark-prone areas.

Avoid thrashing and leg kicking. Smooth swimming movements are less likely to attract sharks.

Do surf or swim in groups. Sharks tend to attack lone individuals.

Don't wear bright colors or high-contrast clothes or wetsuits. If you miraculously survive a plane crash and are floating in the ocean wearing a brightly colored life vest, take it off as soon as possible. Shark biologists call this color yum-yum yellow.

ADVANCED

Most shark attacks begin with a warning bite. Sharks are territorial and may want you (a potential competitor and threat) to leave the area. Or they may mistake you for their preferred prey (sea lion or seal).

If you are attacked, make yourself big and demonstrate strength. Stay upright, facing the shark, and maintain eye contact.

Fight like hell. A shark's nose, eyes and gills are extremely sensitive. A sharp blow or jab in those areas may cause a shark to back off. Never play dead.

Use a knife or any blunt object to strike a shark. Your (edible) hands and feet should be used as a last resort only.

If a shark bites once and swims away, the priority is to stop any bleeding and get out of the water. Don't worry about a second attack. Fatal shark encounters are usually due to the initial injury.

Carry shark repellent. The liquid or spray made from putrefied shark flesh is highly effective at repelling nearby sharks. You can buy it online for less than $30.

HIKE THE INCA TRAIL

WHAT It's a crazy place to build a city, but there it is
WHERE Machu Picchu, Peru
BRAG FACTOR Medium
LIKELIHOOD TO DIE Low
BEST TIME TO GO May–September
PHYSICAL DIFFICULTY Medium
COST $$–$$$

Machu Picchu is the world's most famous Inca archaeological ruin, and rightly so. The setting is beyond photogenic: As the early morning clouds lift, the scale and sheer audacity of the ruins deeply impress. They're built on a notch between two Andean peaks, nearly 8,000 feet above sea level, encircled and protected by a thicket of forest-clad mountains. Below, the jungle flows into the lowlands.

Machu Picchu includes more than 150 buildings built in the 1450s during the reign of Inca emperor Pachacuti. The exact purpose of the site is unknown; it's either a temple complex or a country estate for the emperor. Or maybe an astronomical site. Or perhaps a pilgrimage destination. All we know for sure is that the city was largely abandoned in the late 1500s, likely due to an outbreak of smallpox.

The city was never quite "lost." Small groups of Inca farmers have always lived at and around Machu Picchu. But it certainly stayed hidden for centuries. Remote and well camouflaged, Machu Picchu was never found by Spanish conquistadors and remained unknown in the west until explorer (and Yale University professor) Hiram Bingham III encountered Machu Picchu in 1911.

Today the well-preserved ruins attract more than 1.2 million annual visitors from tourists who saunter out of luxury buses parked choc-a-bloc at the ruins' entrance to backpackers who hike the twenty-mile Inca Trail or one of the alternative trails to Machu Picchu.

Since 2001, the Peruvian government has limited the number of daily visitors to Machu Picchu at 2,500, and requires hikers to book with a local operator. Do-it-yourself treks are not really an option on the main Inca Trail. Fortunately, the Inca were master builders. Many of their ancient roads through the Andes still exist and form a network of alternate routes to Machu Picchu to this day.

The Basics

There is only one hotel in Machu Picchu. All other visitors come up from the nearby town of Aguas Calientes. Buses regularly run from town to the ruins. Or skip the bus and hike the steep forty-five-minute trail to Machu Picchu.

Most visitors rush to arrive before dawn in order to be one of the first four hundred people eligible to climb the famed Huayna Picchu (the iconic peak towering above Machu Picchu, which takes three hours round-trip) or Machu Picchu Mountain (at the opposite end of the site, twice as tall as Huayna Picchu and less crowded).

Machu Picchu entrance tickets must be purchased in advance; they are not sold on site. Purchase them online from the Peruvian Ministry of Culture or a licensed online reseller, or in person at the Ministry of Culture offices in Cusco or Aguas Calientes. Tickets cost $50 (basic entry) or $65 (combo tickets including Huayna Picchu or Machu Picchu Mountain).

Many treks depart from the town of Cusco. To limit damage to the trails, the Peruvian government requires all hikers to travel with a licensed guide. They provide tents and food; you bring boots, a backpack, and a sleeping bag.

The iconic and popular Inca Trail follows the original Inca road from the valley up to the summit of Machu Picchu. The scenery is superb and there are plenty of worthy Inca sites en route. Note that the government limits access to the Inca Trail to five hundred people per day, guides and porters included. Permits for the peak summer season sell out months in advance. The trek takes four days, with a short hike on the last day timed to arrive in Machu Picchu before sunrise. Expect to pay $700 and up.

If you can't secure a permit for the Inca Trail, or are simply put off by the crowds, consider one of the alternate routes to Machu Picchu. They are unpermitted, less touristy, and often more affordable than the classic Inca Trail. The five-day Salkantay Trek, voted one of National Geographic's Top 25 Treks in the World, is a challenging route that scales Salkantay Pass (15,091 feet; 6,271 meters). The less strenuous Lares Trek combines Machu Picchu with a chance to visit local Andean communities that have hardly changed in the past hundred years. The Choquequirao Trek—the longest and toughest in the region—is often combined with Machu Picchu, making it the ultimate archaeological trekking experience.

Machu Picchu is busiest May through September. July and August, the peak tourist season, coincide with the not-quite-so-wet season (Machu Picchu doesn't have a dry season—just a less wet season).

November through April is the true rainy season. The months of November and April themselves are ideal if you want to avoid the heaviest crowds and the heaviest rains.

Note that the Inca Trail closes every February for restoration work.

THINGS TO KNOW

- × Machu Picchu is something of an engineering wonder. The Inca did not use draft animals, iron tools, or wheels. And yet they somehow moved vast amounts of stone and earth to create the foundations of Machu Picchu (more than 60 percent of the construction at Machu Picchu is underground, out of sight).

- × We may never know why the Inca built Machu Picchu. But we do know the site's location was strongly influenced by nearby *apus*, or "holy mountains." The orientation of the Temple of the Sun, for example, points due south and directly through the famous Intihuatana stone, which itself accurately tracks the two equinoxes. Twice a year, the sun sits directly over the Intihuatana stone, creating no shadow.

- × The Inca spoke Quechua, one of the three official languages of modern Peru (along with Spanish and Aymara). Ancient Quechua lacked an alphabetic writing system, so the Inca used *quipu*, or "knot strings," to communicate. Colored strings and several hundred knots recorded dates, statistics, taxes, and even key episodes from traditional folk stories.

TRUE OR FALSE? Both corn and potatoes are native to Peru.

False. Corn was domesticated in multiple spots in the Americas. Only the potato is a true Peruvian original.

CONQUER THE LOST WORLD

WHAT Explore Angel Falls and the tablelands by foot, canoe or airplane

WHERE Canaima National Park, Venezuela

BRAG FACTOR Medium

LIKELIHOOD TO DIE Low

BEST TIME TO GO October–December

PHYSICAL DIFFICULTY Medium

COST $$$–$$$$

Sir Arthur Conan Doyle's classic 1912 adventure novel, *The Lost World*, was inspired by Venezuela's very own "lost world."

No, there aren't any of Doyle's dinosaurs or prehistoric creatures roaming the Venezuelan jungles. Instead, the dense jungles of southeastern Venezuela have *tepui*, "table-top mountains" that, for millennia, were isolated from the forests and savannahs that buffet the tepui like vast green oceans.

The most famous tepui is Mount Roraima, a massive tableland encircled on all sides by 2,000-foot cliffs rising abruptly above the rainforest, like an immense fortress in the clouds. Mount Roraima, home to a half-dozen plants and animals found nowhere else on Earth, is a bizarre landscape of blackened stone pinnacles and marshy ponds. In the wet season it rains daily, sending torrents of water cascading over the cliffs.

Waterfalls are everywhere in the tablelands; nearby Auyán-tepui is the source of the world's tallest waterfall, mighty Angel Falls (3,212 feet; 979 meters). It's more than fifteen times higher than Niagara Falls, 800 feet taller than Yosemite Falls, and taller than three Eiffel Towers standing end to end. Angel Falls is so high that most of the billowing water dissipates into mist before ever reaching the ground below.

It is possible to see Angel Falls by plane or helicopter; however, its jaw-dropping scale is best experienced on a *curiara,* "canoe," from below, paddling up Churún River and the great towering walls of Cañón del Diablo, "Devil's Canyon."

The tepui are part of Venezuela's mountainous Canaima National Park. The location is remote—160 miles from the nearest city, Ciudad Bolívar, and more than a thousand miles from the Venezuelan capital, Caracas—and the tepui themselves are not easy to explore. You must fly over the tabletops or sail up the Churún River and then climb them. Either way, it's an adventure worthy of a "lost world."

The Basics

There are many options for exploring the tepui of Canaima National Park. If you're truly motivated and have the stamina, ten- and eleven-day treks reach the summit of either Mount Roraima or Auyán-tepui (your choice) and include round-trip transfers from Caracas. Expect to pay at least $3,500 per person.

Shorter tours, usually four or five days in length, include treks among the tepui (usually no summiting) and a canoe trip to the base of Angel Falls, for about $2,000 per person.

It's tough to experience the lost world in fewer than three days; but an express option includes a puddle-jumper flight to Canaima National Park, a boat transfer to Anatoly Island, and a canoe ride to Cañón del Diablo before a hike up to the base of Angel Falls. You're back in Caracas on the third day and your wallet is $1,200 lighter.

If you come for the waterfalls, Venezuela's wet season (May to November) is the best time to visit. November and December are especially popular, as the rainy season is just ending and the water levels are still high.

During the dry season, most waterfalls, including Angel Falls, slow considerably. The Churún River may be unapproachable by boat at the peak of dry season.

THINGS TO KNOW

- Angel Falls wasn't discovered until 1933, when Jimmy Angel, an American pilot in search of gold, flew over them. He returned four years later, crash-landing his plane on Auyán-tepui and surviving an arduous eleven-day hike back to civilization.

- The first recorded ascent of Mount Roraima was in 1884 by Everard im Thurn, a British adventurer and colonial administrator. Thurn's original route is the same one used today by hikers.

- In the local Pemon language, Auyán-tepui means "Devil Mountain." More than thirty thousand Pemons still live in the shadow of Auyán-tepui and believe it's home to an evil spirit who lurks in wait for them in the dense forest, taking the form of a poisonous snake in the underbrush or a sharp branch that pokes them in the eye.

TRUE OR FALSE? Venezuela is officially known as the Bolivarian Republic of Venezuela.

True. Simón Bolívar, the driving force behind South America's liberation from Spanish colonial rule, was born in Venezuela. Its currency is named after him, too: the bolívar fuerte.

SUMMIT STOK KANGRI

WHAT India's most famous mountain trek
WHERE Ladakh, India
BRAG FACTOR High
LIKELIHOOD TO DIE Medium
BEST TIME TO GO July–September
PHYSICAL DIFFICULTY Extreme
COST $

There are many summits in the Himalayas, but Stok Kangri stands out for so many reasons. At 20,187 feet, it is the highest trekkable summit in India. It is by no means an easy trail to the top, and yet, people come from all over the world to climb it. Summiting Stok Kangri is one of those glamorous bucket-list experiences because it is a difficult trek in one of the world's most beautiful mountain ranges.

Nearly all treks up Stok Kangri begin in Leh, the capital of the Indian state of Ladakh and perhaps the most hospitable spot on Earth. You can't walk far in Leh without a shopkeeper or farmer greeting you with a wide smile and a musical "*jullay!*" (pronounced joo-lay), an all-purpose word for hello, goodbye, and thanks.

From Leh, you cross the Indus River and climb up and over high passes and high desert valleys, stopping at small Ladakhi villages and the occasional Buddhist monastery for tea and yak milk. Then it's on to Stok village (11,800 feet) and an overnight to help altitude acclimatization in Chang Ma (13,087 feet). Another day of hiking and another overnight to assist acclimatization, this time in Mankorma (14,200 feet). You're approaching base camp (16,300 feet) and its colorful tent minicity, where safety-conscious trekkers rest for two days before attempting the summit (20,187 feet).

This final climb is tough. Most groups leave around 11 P.M., in the bitter cold, buffeted by high winds, and reach the summit the next day around 9 A.M. and are rewarded with sweeping views far above the glorious Zanskar and Indus valleys. The hike back to base camp takes four or five hours. You made it.

The Basics

Be warned: Stok Kangri is dangerous. While it does not require mountaineering skills, it is almost impossible for inexperienced trekkers to conquer the summit. It should not be your first summit attempt in the Himalayas.

You need a full week or more to safely reach the summit of Stok Kangri. Some climbers shave off a few days in order to reduce the cost. This is a bad idea. Your body needs proper acclimatization to handle the lower volume of oxygen in the high-altitude air.

You must also come prepared for extreme weather. A bright sunny day can turn into a blizzard in just a few minutes. Crampons are a must, along with quality clothing and camping gear. You're in the middle of nowhere, far from supplies and support.

The trekking season in Ladakh is short, from late June to early October. After that, temperatures drop and snow accumulates on mountain passes.

There is no requirement to hire a guide or join an organized trek. However, it is a wise investment, costing from $1,000 to $2,000 for seven- or ten-day itineraries from Leh. Only highly experienced and fully equipped mountaineers should attempt a solo summit of Stok Kangri.

THINGS TO KNOW

- × Spend at least two days above 15,000 feet before attempting to summit Stok Kangri.

- × Acclimatization is not a nice-to-have, it's a must-have. It's not uncommon for poorly prepared trekkers to make it to base camp or just beyond, only to stop and turn back with bleeding noses and dizziness.

- × Leh's travel season is short, but it's intense. Visitor numbers have boomed in recent years thanks to a relative calm in tensions between India and Pakistan over the neighboring, and hotly contested, state of Jammu and Kashmir.

TRUE OR FALSE? Ladakh is home to the world's only kung fu Buddhist nunnery.

True. Ladakh's Drukpa nunnery follows a branch of feminist Buddhism that encourages nuns to train in the martial art of kung fu. It also allows them to seek enlightenment on a par with monks. Kill Bill: Volume 3, anybody?

HOW TO COPE WITH ALTITUDE SICKNESS

BASIC

Altitude sickness is a risk at 8,000 feet above sea level and higher. This is the point at which oxygen levels in the air decrease significantly.

Ascend slowly to allow your body to adjust to the reduced oxygen levels. This is called acclimatization. The rule of thumb is to go no more than 1,000 feet of altitude gain per day, and never go above 9,000 feet on your first day in the mountains.

Climb high, sleep low. Oxygen levels in your blood are lowest at night. Plan your day to hike to high elevations and descend to lower altitudes for sleeping. And do not sleep more than 2,000 feet above the altitude you slept the previous night.

Don't drink alcohol, don't exercise. Both stress your blood's oxygen levels. Avoid both for the first forty-eight hours at higher altitudes.

Hydrate. You must drink twice the normal amount of water to maintain hydration at altitudes above 8,000 feet. Minimize salt intake.

Eat foods rich in potassium. They help your body acclimatize more quickly. Avocado, banana, broccoli, cantaloupe, celery, chocolate, granola, and potato are all potassium-rich foods.

Spend an extra day acclimatizing for every 3,000 feet you ascend above 9,000 feet.

ADVANCED

Take an altitude-sickness medicine such as acetazol-amide (a.k.a. Diamox). It prevents and treats symptoms by increasing urine production and respiratory ventilation, both of which support oxygen exchange in the blood stream.

Alternatively, ibuprofen can relieve altitude headaches, while ginger in any form (chews, capsules, or tea) calms a nauseated stomach.

As a last resort, take sildenafil (a.k.a. Viagra). Erectile dysfunction and altitude sickness both respond to drugs that expand blood vessels and improve blood flow.

In South America, coca leaves are used locally to prevent altitude sickness. They are effective chewed or in tea. Note that coca leaves are illegal in the United States and will likely result in a positive test for cocaine use.

Acute mountain sickness (AMS) is the mildest form of altitude sickness. Symptoms—which include headache, nausea, fatigue, and appetite loss—typically fade within seventy-two hours.

If you have symptoms, move to lower ground immediately. The rule of thumb is to descend 1,500 feet at a time, until your symptoms disappear.

If you are confused, lack coordination, and are extremely fatigued, you may have high-altitude cerebral edema (HACE), the extreme form of AMS. Descend immediately to avoid a life-threatening blood clot in your lungs. Above 14,000 feet, if you are short of breath, coughing continuously, or blacking out, you likely have high-altitude pulmonary edema (HAPE). Consider this a medical emergency. Descend immediately and begin oxygen therapy if possible.

FIND HAPPINESS IN THE HIMALAYAS

WHAT Don't worry, be happy
WHERE Bhutan
BRAG FACTOR Medium
LIKELIHOOD TO DIE Low
BEST TIME TO GO March–May or September–October
PHYSICAL DIFFICULTY Medium
COST $$–$$$

This remote Himalayan kingdom has long been known for its pursuit of balance between the spiritual and the material. Bhutan's king even coined a phrase for it back in 1979, calling it "Gross National Happiness," a philosophy that measures the collective happiness of a nation through its economic self-reliance, environmental conservation, cultural preservation, and good governance. These are the Four Pillars of Happiness as enshrined in the country's 2008 constitution.

Bhutan's long-standing policy of isolationism—fewer than sixty thousand foreigners are allowed to visit each year—helps to preserve traditional lifestyles and Himalayan culture. Bhutan has no beggars, few Bhutanese live in true poverty, television and the Internet are encountered rarely, and more than 50 percent of the country is protected as a national park. People earn a living wage and are generally happy. Clearly the Bhutanese are doing something right.

For westerners, Bhutan has always been difficult to visit. The government sets minimum daily spending requirements. And it requires all treks, whether you've come for a day hike or a grueling month-long adventure, to be arranged through a local agent.

As long as you are willing to accommodate these policies, Bhutan is truly awesome in the infinitely mesmerizing, hard-to-fathom, standing-there-with-your-mouth-agape use of the word.

The Basics

Bhutan's "high value, low impact" tourism policy means every visitor must pay a minimum daily fee of $250 (March—May and September—November) or $200 (all other times). There's an additional daily surcharge for solo travelers ($40) and groups of two ($30 per person). All visitors must book through Bhutanese tour operators (or their international partners) to gain entry.

On one hand, the minimum fee is annoying. On the other hand, it covers nearly all your costs in Bhutan, including three-star accommodation (you can pay more for premium accommodation), all meals, a licensed Bhutanese guide for your stay, all internal transport, and all camping gear for trekking. On any trek in Bhutan, you are accompanied by a guide, cook, and a few horses to carry gear, all at no additional cost.

Trekking in neighboring Nepal is all about tea houses (mountain guesthouses that feed and shelter independent trekkers). Bhutan has no equivalent. Villages and settlements are few and far between on Bhutan's trekking routes.

Among treks, the three-day Bumthang Owl Trek is one of the shortest in Bhutan. The six-day Druk Path Trek is another good, short-ish option, blending stunning mountain landscapes with a chance to visit ancient temples and monasteries.

The eight- to eleven-day Jhomolhari Trek is one of Bhutan's most popular. It's a moderately difficult route that crosses both Bhonte La pass (16,000 feet) and Takhung La pass (14,829 feet), with near-continuous views of spectacular Mt. Jomolhari (24,035 feet).

The fourteen-day Laya-Gasa Trek is considered the most scenic in Bhutan, carving a path through 130 miles of unspoiled mountain landscapes. And then there's the Snowman Trek, Bhutan's most famous route and widely considered to be the most difficult trek in the world. You need a minimum of twenty-five days (thirty days is more realistic) to climb the eleven high-altitude passes along the remote, largely unpopulated border between Bhutan and Tibet.

Bhutan's climate is dominated by the Indian monsoon. The best months for trekking are March to May and September to October. If you're attempting the Snowman Trek, October is the best month.

THINGS TO KNOW

* Until 1974, all foreigners (excluding people from neighboring India) were barred from entering Bhutan.

* Smoking is illegal in Bhutan. Chalk it up to improving gross national happiness.

* Bhutan's true secret to happiness? A good night's sleep. Well-rested people live longer, healthier, and more productive lives. According to national surveys, more than two-thirds of Bhutanese sleep a minimum of eight hours per night. Compare that to the United States, where forty percent of adults sleep six hours or fewer, leaving us tired and cranky and prone to numerous diseases.

* International Day of Happiness? It's recognized by the United Nations and celebrated on March 20.

* Gangkhar Puensum (24,836 feet) is Bhutan's tallest peak and likely the highest unclimbed mountain in the world. Many have tried, but no one has reached the summit. The government of Bhutan has since prohibited the climbing of peaks higher than 6,000 meters (19,568 feet). Unless the policy changes, Gangkhar Puensum is likely to remain unclimbed.

What is the unhappiest country on Earth?

The Central African Republic, according to the United Nations' most recent World Happiness Report.

DRIVE TO THE WORLD'S END

WHAT Next stop, oblivion
WHERE McMurdo Station, Antarctica
BRAG FACTOR High
LIKELIHOOD TO DIE Medium
BEST TIME TO GO Antarctic summer (December–February)
PHYSICAL DIFFICULTY High
COST $$$$

McMurdo Station is a living monument to science. This minicity in the Antarctic, on the south tip of Ross Island, is the year-round home of a thousand dedicated researchers and support staff. These men and women brave the weather and the isolation in order to gather data, documenting what it means to stand atop a mile-thick ice sheet on a planet that is quickly warming.

They also live at the beginning of the world's most southerly road. It's officially the McMurdo–South Pole Highway or, for short, the South Pole Traverse. This hardened-snow road connects McMurdo Station to the Amundsen-Scott South Pole Station, a two-hundred-person science outpost located nearly 2,000 miles away at the very heart of the South Pole.

Most years, sometime between December and February (summertime in the Southern Hemisphere), a few dozen of McMurdo's hardiest load up specially designed sleds with tons of supplies, and head off in oversized tractors to the South Pole. The annual resupply journey takes thirty-five to forty days *each way* and is critical to maintaining a year-round human presence at the South Pole.

Getting to McMurdo simply for fun, as a tourist, ain't gonna happen. However, each year a few hundred civilians are employed as McMurdo Station support staff. While you may not get the experience of driving end-to-end on the South Pole Traverse (few do), a summer or winter stint at McMurdo guarantees at least a walk, run, or even a bike ride on the road leading to the world's very end.

The Basics

The South Pole Traverse is not your typical road. It's not paved. There are no stop lights, rest stops, or gas stations. And there is not a single fast-food drive-thru en route. Instead, it's as barren and bleak as can be. Flags mark the way, though shifting ice and unexpected crevices are common, as are temperatures in the negative 70 degrees and 80 degrees Fahrenheit.

And, of course, there is no emergency roadside service. If you get stuck along its nearly 2,000-mile length, you are well and truly stuck.

Construction began in 2002 and was mostly complete in 2007. The United States funded the project to lower the cost of resupplying the South Pole Station. It also has the added benefit of reducing the carbon footprint of South Pole research; before the road was built, roughly forty flights each summer were required to deliver the necessary fuel and cargo.

How to get there? The best option is to apply for a job on the United States Antarctic Program website; this is the official government agency that screens, hires, and deploys hundreds of dishwashers, cooks, drivers, mechanics, plumbers, and the like to McMurdo and other Antarctic research stations each year.

THINGS TO KNOW

× McMurdo Station is a true city, with a harbor, airfields, a heliport, and more than a hundred buildings. It also has the Antarctic's only ATM.

- Can you bike to the world's end? Yes! In 2013, a rocket scientist *and* bicycle enthusiast named Maria Leijerstam pedaled a recumbent three-wheeler more than 420 miles, over ten days, on the South Pole Traverse. In doing so, she became the first person to arrive at the South Pole by bike.

- Besides looking for people with useful skills like cooking and driving, McMurdo Station invites the occasional artist as part of its Antarctic Writers & Artists Program. That is how filmmaker Werner Herzog spent seven weeks at McMurdo Station in 2006, shooting what became his well-received 2007 documentary *Encounters at the End of the World*.

TRUE OR FALSE? McMurdo Station was once powered by nuclear energy.

True. Starting in 1962, McMurdo Station used a nuclear reactor the size of an oil drum to produce all its power. Safety concerns caused the US Navy to decommission the nuclear reactor in 1972.

SPEND TEN DAYS IN SPACE

WHAT No joke You can book a room at the International Space Station
WHERE International Space Station
BRAG FACTOR Extreme
LIKELIHOOD TO DIE Medium
BEST TIME TO GO When you can afford it
PHYSICAL DIFFICULTY Extreme
COST $$$$$$$$$$$$$

For more than a decade, a handful of private companies have offered suborbital Earth flights that—while not cheap—are affordable in the way that a Ferrari or Bugatti sports car is affordable to the ultra-, mega-, superrich.

But what about spending time in space? Or sleeping in space? Or maybe donning a pressure suit for your own private spacewalk? Impossible.

And yet, it *is* possible. To date, seven private citizens have flown into space and spent ten days or more living and working on the International Space Station (ISS). The company Space Adventures has arranged every one of these flights, in partnership with Russia's space agency.

It is completely legal and legitimate. As long as you are rich beyond belief and in decent physical shape, Space Adventures will prepare you to be an astronaut: zero-gravity flights, centrifuge training, supersonic jet flights and more, mostly at the Yuri Gagarin Cosmonaut Training Center in Star City, Russia. Mission preparation, tailored to each aspiring astronaut, lasts roughly six months.

Then it's go time. You fly to the ISS on a Russian Soyuz spacecraft, dock and transfer to the station, and spend the next ten days living and working alongside the ISS's six permanent astronauts. As a civilian, you are free to spend your time aboard the ISS as you choose.

Most of Space Adventures' clients design their missions to include assisting in space science . . . and taking plenty of selfies, floating weightlessly, while marveling at the Earth below. A Russian Soyuz spacecraft ferries you back to Earth at the end of your time in space.

The ISS is an orbital laboratory and the only continuously occupied outpost in space. It is roughly 250 miles above the Earth's surface, traveling at more than 17,500 miles per hour. It circles our home planet every ninety minutes, offering truly one-of-a-kind perspectives on the lonely blue dot we call home.

The Basics

All flights to and from the ISS are aboard Russia's Soyuz TMA-M spacecraft, currently the only craft transporting people and supplies to the station. Four trips a year are scheduled, accommodating a maximum of three astronauts per flight. Russia's Soyuz program has an excellent safety record.

The ISS itself, with a wingspan of more than 300 feet, is roughly the same size (inside) as a Boeing 777 aircraft. A permanent crew of six astronauts manages the station's science programs. So far, seven civilian astronauts have spent ten days at the station, all under the Space Adventures program. Dennis Tito, an American entrepreneur, was the very first Space Adventures client to go to ISS, in 2001.

The cost to spend ten days on the ISS? The current rate is $50 million and, believe it or not, there is a waiting list.

THINGS TO KNOW

- To date, only 540 people have traveled to space. Space Adventures would like to double that number in the next ten years.

- The largest hurdle to commercializing space is the cost of the rocket launch. Government-sponsored launches in the United States and Russia cost $300 million to $400 million apiece. Recent breakthroughs in reusable rockets by companies such as Jeff Bezos's Blue Origin and Elon Musk's SpaceX will decrease launch costs to roughly $50 million or $60 million. By the mid-2020s, a trip to space or a stay on the ISS may cost just a few hundred thousand dollars; at least that's the hope of commercial spaceflight companies.

✕ The ISS itself is the result of over twenty-five years of international cooperation between the United States, Russia, Japan, Canada, and major European countries. It is the single-most expensive science project in history, costing more than $150 billion to build and operate. Compare that to the $2.5 billion NASA spent on its hugely successful Mars lander program, or the $10 billion it costs to run the Large Hadron Collider in CERN, and you can see why governments are eager to recoup some of ISS's costs through space tourism.

✕ Want to add a spacewalk to your ISS experience? No problem. For an extra $15 million, Space Adventures will allow clients to take a ninety-minute spacewalk from the ISS.

✕ Fly to the moon? Yup. Space Adventures is prebooking lunar missions that circumnavigate the moon at altitudes below 80 miles. Seats on a moon-bound Russian spacecraft (two paying customers, one professional Russian cosmonaut) are priced at $150 million each.

TRUE OR FALSE? The first American in orbit peed his space suit.

True. Alan Shephard's groundbreaking 1961 orbit of Earth, when he became the first American and second person ever in space, was meant to last just fifteen minutes. Numerous delays kept him on the launch pad for hours. Nobody planned ahead for the "astronaut urgently needs to urinate" scenario. Eventually mission control allowed Shephard to pee in his own space suit.

2

Adventures for Adrenaline Junkies

*Higher, faster, farther.
These twenty-three adventures
are for people who crave heart-
pounding experiences on land,
air, or sea.*

SURF A VOLCANO

WHAT Just like surfing . . . but on razor-sharp lava rocks
WHERE León, Nicaragua
BRAG FACTOR Medium
LIKELIHOOD TO DIE Medium
BEST TIME TO GO November–May
PHYSICAL DIFFICULTY High
COST $

It's kinda like surfing. It's kinda like sandboarding. And it's kinda like nothing else you've ever seen.

Volcano surfers use gravity to propel themselves down the rocky, barren slopes of a volcano, while standing on flimsy wooden planks. The sport was invented in the early 2000s by a National Geographic Channel filmmaker on the slopes of Vanuatu's Mt. Yasur. Since then, volcano surfing has developed a hardcore base of fans, even though it's undeniably dangerous. Don't inhale poisonous volcanic gas, don't fall on jagged lava rocks, don't get nailed by a belch of molten lava. . . .

Volcano surfing, or boarding, has also single-handedly transformed tourism in Nicaragua. The country is home to the sport's unofficial top challenge, the active volcano Cerro Negro, which towers more than 2,300 feet above the city of León.

The volcano, which last erupted in the late 1990s, is perfect for volcano boarding because its cone is covered with small, penny-sized rocks. It's like a steep slope covered in razor-sharp marbles, just begging you to ride down or surf it, at speeds up to 50 miles per hour, on a rickety wooden sled with no brakes.

We said volcano boarding was a rush of adrenaline; we never said it was a *smart* idea.

The Basics

It's difficult to travel in Nicaragua without hearing about volcano boarding. It's literally impossible to step foot in the city of León without a half-dozen guides imploring you to sign up for a volcano-boarding adventure on the slopes of Cerro Negro.

The hike up the mountain takes an hour. Then it's go time: you, a plywood sled, and more than 1,600 downhill feet of volcano. Runs last five minutes or so, depending on your speed (and how many times you crash).

You have the option to stand up or sit down on the sled. However, since you can't reliably control the sled's direction or speed, consider sitting down. You'll go faster. And it hurts less when you (inevitably) fall off your board.

Crash suits (more like dirty overalls), goggles, and leather gloves are offered to all riders—please, please, please wear them. Volcano boarding is dangerous. Each year, people are seriously injured and hospitalized from injuries suffered when they lose control of their sleds. Exercise extreme caution if you decide to try it. If all goes well and you survive the first run, you can hike back up for a second try.

From León, it's a forty-five-minute overland drive to Cerro Negro. Operators charge $25 and up for the experience.

THINGS TO KNOW

- × Daryn Webb, the original owner of Nicaragua's Bigfoot Hostel, pioneered the sport's early boards, testing everything from upside-down picnic tables to old mattresses. Eventually he settled on a toboggan-like sled made of wood.

- × It's possible to volcano board in Costa Rica and Hawaii, but there's no denying Nicaragua is the sport's main hub.

✗ Volcano boarding has transformed the tourist economy in León. More than a dozen operators cater to the ten thousand visitors who volcano board each year. Guides can earn more than $500 per month, which is double the local average salary.

TRUE OR FALSE? There are twenty volcanoes erupting right now, as you read this.

True. On average, twenty volcanoes around the globe are spewing molten lava at any given moment. The majority, however, are underwater volcanoes that you never see.

Adventure Skill

HOW TO TREAT CUTS AND LACERATIONS

BASIC

Clean your hands, then thoroughly clean your wound.

Make sure the wound is free of foreign objects (gently remove if there are any).

Apply antibacterial ointment or rubbing alcohol, then cover with a bandage.

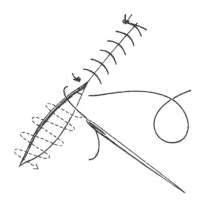

ADVANCED

If the wound will not stay closed, you may need to stitch it closed.

This is best performed by a doctor; when that's not possible, at minimum you need a sterilized needle and suture material such as fishing line or very thin string.

Clean the wound and your hands, and sterilize the needle if possible.

Thread the needle and start suturing from the center of the wound.

Leave one-eighth inch between loops and tie off the knot at both ends.

Repeat on the other half of the wound, again starting from the center.

Bandage and monitor for infection.

CHASE A TORNADO

WHAT Yes, storm chasing is a thing
WHERE Tornado Alley, USA
BRAG FACTOR High
LIKELIHOOD TO DIE Low (high for novice chasers)
BEST TIME TO GO March–June
PHYSICAL DIFFICULTY Low
COST $$–$$$

Tornadoes are one of the most powerful—and deadly—forces on Earth. Intense lighting. Hail. Winds in excess of 100 miles per hour. In the United States alone, more than 1,800 rapidly spinning windstorms touch down each year, carving paths of destruction and killing hundreds of people.

Despite the dangers, some people actually look forward to tornado season. They're known as "storm chasers"—people who spend hours at a time tracking major storms and doing their very best to place themselves in the path of a deadly tornado.

Why?

Because standing in the path of a tornado is the only way to see it up close and personal, in all its explosive and violent glory. It's what motivates storm chasers. It's what they live for.

Needless to say, storm chasing involves driving. And waiting. And more driving. Storms are unpredictable, and often happen in sparsely populated areas in the middle of nowhere. Don't bother with storm chasing if spending hours in a car is not your idea of fun.

The Basics

Tornadoes in the United States are most common in northern Texas, Oklahoma, Kansas, and Nebraska—the so-called Tornado Alley where storm chasers monitor severe weather in hopes of locating a nearby storm to follow.

Low cost do-it-yourself storm chasing is possible; however, storms are deadly and it's never a good idea to do something potentially life-threatening without proper preparation. Go with an experienced storm chaser who knows what he or she is doing.

While there is no formal training required to be a storm chaser, some people make a career of it and offer guided tours of Tornado Alley during peak storm season (March through June). The typical itinerary lasts six to ten days in customized vehicles loaded with high-tech radar and the latest satellite communications gear. The cost is $2,500 and up.

THINGS TO KNOW

* In Tornado Alley, the most popular storm to chase is a supercell thunderstorm. Its compact structure creates the iconic and easy-to-spot cumulonimbus clouds that tower high above the plains. Its rotation produces strong and long-lived tornadoes.

* About three out of ten supercell thunderstorms produce tornadoes. Supercells typically move from southwest to northeast.

* For DIY storm chasers, the best place to base yourself is Wichita, Kansas. The state experiences the largest number of tornadoes per year, and from Wichita you have easy highway access to Oklahoma and southern Nebraska.

✖ If you're balking at the high cost of a guided storm chase, keep in mind that DIY storm chasing is not free. Factor in the cost of renting a car or driving your own vehicle, fuel (a tank per day), food and lodging, and $2,500 for six days of a guided tour is more palatable.

What's the longest path of destruction, measured in miles, of a tornado in the United States?

More than 235 miles. The path was left in 1925 by the Tri-State Tornado, considered the deadliest in US history with more than 690 fatalities.

HOW TO SURVIVE A TORNADO IN A CAR

BASIC

If you see a distant tornado while driving, immediately drive away from the storm.

Seek shelter in the nearest building.

If the tornado is approaching and no shelter is available, drive at right angles away from the tornado as fast as possible.

ADVANCED

If you're caught inside a car, park as quickly as possible out of the traffic lanes.

Stay inside with the seatbelt fastened.

Keep your head down (below the windows) and cover yourself with a blanket or coat.

Do not hide in the trunk; it's safer to stay in the car with a seatbelt on.

If there's low ground nearby (ditch, irrigation gulley, etc.), it's better to exit the car and lie down there, covering the back of your head with your hands.

FALL TO EARTH

WHAT It's more like a suicide mission than a sport
WHERE Fayetteville, West Virginia
BRAG FACTOR Medium
LIKELIHOOD TO DIE Uncomfortably high
BEST TIME TO GO October
PHYSICAL DIFFICULTY Medium
COST $$

Is there any adventure riskier than BASE jumping? Probably not.

The idea is crazy: Leap from a fixed object wearing a parachute or a flying wingsuit (a flying wingsuit?!). The experience of falling to the ground provides a short, intense, burst of adrenaline. Apparently, it's addictive. Once you start BASE jumping, it's hard to stop. Unless you die.

BASE is an acronym for four types of fixed objects that participants jump from: building, antenna, span (i.e. bridge), and earth (i.e. cliff or rock face). Because BASE jumpers start from low altitudes, there's little time to deploy a parachute or deal with last-second shifts in wind or jumping conditions. It's the difference between life or death measured in thousandths of a second.

There's no way to sugarcoat it. BASE jumping is far, far more dangerous than skydiving; injury and fatality rates are more than *forty times* higher.

The Basics

BASE jumping is essentially the act of parachuting from fixed objects (as opposed to planes). Because of the danger involved, it is illegal in many places. People often survive jumps only to be arrested on landing.

Bridge Day is the oldest and largest legal BASE jumping event in the world. It's held annually, on the third Saturday in October, in Fayetteville, West Virginia. Hundreds of experienced jumpers attend. A strong emphasis on first-time jumpers means this is one of the few ways to try BASE jumping safely (at least, as safe as BASE jumping can be). Bridge Day offers one-day training courses following by a BASE jump from the event's namesake span, the 876-foot-tall New River Gorge Bridge. It'll set you back around $500.

THINGS TO KNOW

- Filmmaker Carl Boenish was the catalyst behind modern BASE jumping. In 1978, he filmed the first jumps made by parachute from the famous El Capitan rock formation in Yosemite National Park. Unfortunately, he died attempting a BASE jump in Norway.

- Wingsuits allow you to modify your flight trajectory in midair, using minute adjustments of your arms or body. No joke, the first wingsuits were modeled on flying squirrels.

- The first attempt at wingsuit flying was in Paris in 1912, by Franz Reichelt. He fashioned a suit made from a silk parachute stretched across a small wing. Reichelt told guards at the Eiffel Tower he was merely testing the suit on a dummy. Instead, he flight-tested his own invention and—wait for it . . . yes—died on the first attempt.

- The current record for highest building BASE jump is 2,716 feet, achieved by Frenchman Fred Fugen and Vince Reffet at Dubai's Burj Khalifa tower in 2014.

- One of BASE jumping's best marketing assets is James Bond. The fictional British spy has performed at least four jumps, including one from skis and another from the Eiffel Tower.

Mostly false. It allowed BASE jumping in the mid-1990s. That ended after a Space Needle jumper was injured in 1996. Today it is illegal to jump from any building in metro Seattle.

JUMP SKY HIGH

WHAT Two minutes at terminal velocity
WHERE Multiple locations
BRAG FACTOR Sky high!
LIKELIHOOD TO DIE Sky high!
BEST TIME TO GO Year-round
PHYSICAL DIFFICULTY High
COST $$–$$$

HALO skydiving stands for "High Altitude–Low Opening" and basically means you jump from heights greater than Mt. Everest and free-fall for as long as possible, opening your chute at the lowest safe altitude.

This is a great idea if you're in the military. Give the enemy as little time as possible to see you and your Special Forces team coming. For the rest of us, it's frightening as hell.

The civilian version of HALO includes two minutes of free fall either solo or as part of a tandem (two-person) jump team, from altitudes of 30,000 feet or higher. This is more than twice the altitude—and more than three times the duration—achieved in free fall compared to a standard skydive. For high-altitude thrill seekers, HALO jumping is the ultimate adventure.

The Basics

Prepping for a solo HALO jump is serious business. First-time jumpers typically perform one or two dives from lower altitudes to get familiar with the required high-altitude gear: ballistic helmet, oxygen mask, oxygen regulator, full-body flight suit, gloves, and emergency bailout gear.

First-time tandem jumpers skip the test dives but are required to don all the same equipment. A full day of on-the-ground safety training is generally required.

One-day HALO tandem jumps are regularly offered in Hawaii, Alaska, and Tennessee. The programs last a full day and typically cost $1,500 and up. Solo jumps cost less ($800 and up) and are easier to find, because certified solo-HALO operators exist around the United States. However, solo jumping requires a longer time commitment, often two to three days.

THINGS TO KNOW

- ✕ HALO jumps start at such eye-popping altitudes, typically above 30,000 feet, that all HALO jumps require special approval from the Federal Aviation Administration (FAA).

- ✕ The air temperature at 30,000 feet? It hovers around a bone-chilling, skin-searing negative 35 degrees Fahrenheit.

- ✕ The record altitude achieved in HALO skydiving is a mind-bending 135,890 feet, set by Google employee Alan Eustace in 2014.

- ✕ The HALO speed record belongs to the Red Bull Stratos project and extreme athlete Felix Baumgartner, who unexpectedly blasted past the sound barrier and hit 833 miles per hour (Mach 1.24!!) when he jumped from a helium-filled balloon at 128,100 feet in 2012.

TRUE OR FALSE? When Alan Eustace jumped from more than 135,000 feet in 2014, he was jumping to Earth from the edge of outer space.

False. The Earth-space boundary is much, much higher up, at 330,000 feet.

TRAIN AS A WING WALKER

> **WHAT** Gymnastics in a hurricane
> **WHERE** Sequim, Washington
> **BRAG FACTOR** High
> **LIKELIHOOD TO DIE** Medium
> **BEST TIME TO GO** July–September
> **PHYSICAL DIFFICULTY** Medium
> **COST** $$

Who hasn't fantasized about flying high in the sky among the clouds, wind blowing in your face? We all have.

Now raise your hand if you've fantasized about doing that . . . while walking on the wings of an airplane . . . flying upside down. Are there any hands raised?

It's called wing walking, and it works just the way sounds. Take off in a biplane, climb a few thousand feet, then walk out onto the wing and strap in. You're now ready to perform tricks from the wing-walking repertoire (handstands and acrobatic dance moves) as the plane rolls, spins, and does loop-the-loops.

As a spectator, it's breathtaking. As a performer, it takes strength and concentration. Wing walking is not for people who are easily airsick, or for anybody with a fear of heights. For everybody else, it's a unique experience that you'll be talking about for a long time to come.

Any story that begins with, "Remember that time I was walking on the wing of a plane . . . ?" is a story worth telling.

The Basics

True wing walking is an art form on the decline. Acts pop up occasionally at air shows and state fairs, but don't hold your breath. In an effort to preserve this fading art, pilot and third-generation wing walker Mike Mason runs the only school in the United States dedicated to wing walking. It's less about offering a thrill ride (though don't worry, there are plenty of thrills) and more about exposing people to the art form.

Who knows, maybe some people will make a career of wing walking. Mike and his wife, Marilyn, would be pleased to teach you. According to the Masons, the global community of professional wing walkers is tiny, and the Masons have trained most of them.

The Boeing Stearman biplanes, built originally in the 1930s and '40s, are sturdy barnstorming machines that can handle plenty of g-forces during loops and climbs. They reach a top speed of about 160 miles per hour.

No previous wing walking experience is required. One-day courses cost around $900 and include plenty of time wing walking, plus learning how to climb from cockpit to the upper wing rack (your strapping point) and along the lower wing.

Late summer is the best time of year to fly out of Sequim. It's on the Olympic Peninsula, about two hours by car from Seattle.

THINGS TO KNOW

× The heyday of wing walking was in the 1920s and '30s. That's when barnstormer pilots and aerial stunt people made a living entertaining crowds with breathtaking feats. These "flying circuses" performed at air shows across the country with names like the 13 Black Cats, the Five Blackbirds (an all African American group), and Bugs McGowen's Flying Circus.

- Ormer Locklear is considered the father of aviation aerobatics. He was the first to do a handstand, hang upside down off a wing, and hang below a plane by holding onto a rope ladder—with only his teeth! He also performed the first jump from one plane to another while in midair.

- The beginning of the end of professional wing walking came in 1938, when the US government required all wing walkers to wear parachutes while performing. Those nettlesome government regulations. Drats!

- The Breitling Wingwalkers, a stunt aerobatic team based in England, recently advertised for a full-time wing walker to join the team. Applicants must be no taller than 5 foot 5 inches, weigh less than 120 pounds, and be interested in more than money.

TRUE OR FALSE? Famed aviator Charles Lindbergh began his career in flight as a wing walker.

True. Lindbergh was especially famous for the "double-jump." Wearing two parachutes, he would jump from the wing and pull his first chute. He would then remove it midair, to the horror of crowds below. He would land safely using the second chute.

ENTER THE MONGOL RALLY

WHAT England to Asia in the crappiest car you can buy

WHERE London to Ulan-Ude

BRAG FACTOR High

LIKELIHOOD TO DIE Reasonably high (you've read the race rules, right?)

BEST TIME TO GO July–August

PHYSICAL DIFFICULTY Extreme

COST $$$–$$$$

"The ultimate chaos machine" is how event organizers describe the Mongol Rally. The infamous road race spans 10,000 miles of rough and uncharted roads from London to Ulan-Ude in Russia (originally to Ulan Bator in Mongolia).

Six teams entered the first race in 2004 (four finished). In recent years, the event has proven so popular that a *maximum* of two hundred teams are accepted. If the idea of running the Mongol Rally scratches your itch for madcap adventure, sign up as soon as possible.

There is no set course for the Mongol Rally. Once you start, it's up to you to navigate your way across Europe and Russia to the finish line. Typical routes head east via Moscow or Istanbul, though some teams have diverted as far north as the Arctic Circle and as far south as Iran and Turkmenistan. Most teams take anywhere from six to eight weeks to complete the rally.

Along the way, you'll inevitably break down (more than once), encounter mostly unhelpful police and border agents, and wonder what the hell you are doing driving a crappy car in the middle of nowhere, dirty, tired, and lost.

Inevitably, the unexpected kindness of strangers you encounter on dusty back roads will leave its mark on you. The Mongol Rally is the sort of adventure you'll tell the grandkids about. Or put another way, courtesy of the organizers: "Stories so fucking excellent your friends will be in awe of you for decades to come."

The Basics

The Mongol Rally has few rules. In fact, only three.

First, your car must be what the organizers call "small and shit"—preferably a junker with an engine smaller than one liter (1000cc). The maximum engine size allowed is 1.2 liters (1200cc). Motorcycles are OK, but scooters are preferred.

Second, you're on your own. The organizers like to point out that, if they wanted, they could tell you all about the roads, visa requirements, optimal routes, etc. But they won't. Because it's meant to be an adventure.

Finally, the race is run for charity and each team must raise 1,000 British pounds (roughly $1,300).

For many years, the race's end point was in Ulan Bator, Mongolia (hence the "Mongol Rally" name). However, the rally now passes through Mongolia and ends in Ulan-Ude, Russia. This is to avoid the costs associated with "importing and disposing" of rally vehicles in Mongolia (what, you expected to drive your car back to England?! Ha ha ha ha . . .).

The annual race starts in mid-July on the streets of London. It costs just over $1,000 to enter (less for motorcyclists). Expect to spend an additional few thousand dollars per team on food, fuel, plus the occasional hotel.

THINGS TO KNOW

* The organizers have a good sense of humor, but keep in mind the race is serious and, yes, even dangerous. Race participants have been injured, hospitalized and, in one instance, killed in a car crash.

* It's technically illegal to race cars on public highways in Europe. For this reason, the Mongol Rally is intentionally designed not to have winners or a set course. It's also the reason why there is no on-the-road support or assistance.

* While rules for rally vehicles are strict, there is a comedy exemption to consider. In years past, fire engines and stretch limousines and hearses were allowed because, hey, how often do you see a fire truck bouncing across the steppes of Asia?! Nowadays you need to be even "funnier" to skirt the rules.

* Because of past issues with various governments, vehicles are not allowed to be left or disposed of in Ulan-Ude. Once the Rally is over, you must ship your rally car back to Europe and scrap it there.

TRUE OR FALSE? A British Mongol Rally team in 2008 drove a Mini with an iconic red British telephone booth mounted on top, through eighteen countries.

True. And it wasn't simply for show. Given the Mini's small size, the team stored a month's worth of gear and supplies in the telephone booth.

Adventure Skill

HOW TO BRIBE A POLICE OFFICER OR BORDER GUARD

The most important thing is to accept that, in many parts of the world, bribes are unremarkable, not prosecutable, and simply a part of daily life. It doesn't do any good to get mad about it.

The next important thing to recognize is that, even in countries where bribery is endemic, the bribe-taker and bribe-giver are always performing a graceful duet. Each has their role to play. Know your part.

BASIC

Learn the local euphemisms for bribes. You often pay "a fine" for missing paperwork or a "small fee" in order "to expedite" whatever your situation is.

In some countries, police may ask for "a little gift" (northern Africa) or "a refreshment" (Mexico and Central America) or even "a good coffee" (Iraq).

In countries with double-entendre possibilities, you may be asked for *baksheesh* (can mean both "tip" or "bribe" in India and Pakistan) or *chai* (both "tea" and "bribe" in western Africa).

ADVANCED

Never hand money directly to a bribe-taker, or palm a bill into his or her hand. It's not classy.

Fold bribe money into your passport. Or, if the bribe-taker hands you a note pad or ticket book, insert a few bills and hand it back.

Do not overpay. Know the market price of the bribe-takers' services.

Never ask for change. If, for example, you have only a $20 bill and the bribe-taker expects half that amount, give $20 and be prepared to ask for more, for faster, or for enhanced corrupt services.

RUN CABALLO BLANCO

WHAT A race by, and for, the running people
WHERE Urique, Mexico
BRAG FACTOR High
LIKELIHOOD TO DIE Low
BEST TIME TO GO March
PHYSICAL DIFFICULTY High
COST $

The Rarámuri people are reputed to be the greatest natural runners in the world. They have lived in the Copper Canyons of northern Mexico for centuries, and are capable of running vast distances (up to 100 miles in a day) across rocky mountainsides and through steep canyons with virtually no gear and only the slimmest of footwear.

An American named Micah True became obsessed with the Rarámuri and their culture of running. In 2003, he organized the first long-distance race in the Copper Canyon; in 2006, he invited international runners to participate in what had become a 50-mile ultramarathon event.

That year's race was vividly captured by participant Chris McDougall in his book *Born to Run*. The book transformed Micah True and the Rarámuri into international celebrities, and simultaneously turned the Ultramarathon Caballo Blanco into one of the premiere annual events in long-distance running.

Fortunately, you don't need to be a famous runner to join. All you need to do is show up with a will to run hard over tough terrain.

The Basics

The fifty-mile race begins and ends in the village of Urique, at the bottom of Urique Canyon in the Mexican state of Chihuahua. The course is a twenty-one-mile loop, followed by a second eighteen-mile loop plus a ten-mile run out and back to the village of Guadalupe Coronado, before ending back at the starting line in the town of Urique.

The terrain can be treacherous. It's hilly and rocky, weaving through canyons on dirt tracks and unpaved roads. The race cutoff time is sixteen hours; the fastest runners finish in less than seven hours.

The race, held annually in March, is free to enter. The 2015 race was abruptly canceled due to drug-cartel violence in the area. The race was successfully run the following year and continues on a revised route that, hopefully, skirts the drug cartel's area of control.

It's not easy to reach Urique. By bus, it's twelve hours from the Mexican cities of Chihuahua or Los Mochis.

THINGS TO KNOW

- ✕ Micah True (born Michael Randall Hickman) was nicknamed *caballo blanco,* "white horse," by the Rarámuri.

- ✕ The race was renamed the Ultramarathon Caballo Blanco in Micah True's honor, following his highly publicized 2012 death while running alone in the mountains outside Urique. It's assumed he slipped and fell, and died from exposure.

- ✕ *Rarámuri* is loosely translated as "the running people"; in Spanish they are known as the Tarahumara.

- ✕ Micah True first encountered the Rarámuri in 1993 during the brutal 100-mile Leadville Trail race across the Colorado Rockies. Five Rarámuri entered, wearing loincloths and sandals made from recycled car tires. Against all expectations, a Rarámuri runner won, finishing an hour ahead of everybody else. Most impressive of all? The Rarámuri winner was fifty-five years old.

TRUE OR FALSE? Long-distance athletes who run barefoot are more efficient, and have fewer injuries, compared to runners in shoes.

False. Studies show there is no advantage to running barefoot versus running in lightweight, cushioned shoes. However, it is true that the heavier your shoes, the less efficiently you run.

JAM IN A HOTSPOT

WHAT Run, jump, roll, climb, vault, swing . . .
WHERE A hotspot near you
BRAG FACTOR Medium
LIKELIHOOD TO DIE Medium
BEST TIME TO GO Year-round
PHYSICAL DIFFICULTY High
COST $

Movement is delightful.

This is the insight behind parkour, a full-body training discipline that traces it lineage back to military obstacle courses.

Parkour is about movement, specifically getting from one point to another with no gear or equipment, in the fastest and most efficient way possible. It's a little bit martial art, a little bit modern dance, and a little bit aerial acrobatics. You've probably seen videos of parkour, with men and women in mostly urban settings running, climbing, vaulting, jumping, rolling, and generally using their bodies in ways you never imagined possible. Parkour is mesmerizing to watch.

Parkour is not a sport—at least, not according to its founders. They consider it a philosophy, an art, and a practice (similar to yoga). Competitions are frowned upon. Instead there are parkour "jams" lasting anywhere from a few hours to a few days, where participants gather to hone their parkour practice.

Parkour appeals to people who are keen to develop self-discipline; svelte muscle-hardened bodies and off-the-charts stamina are just icing on the cake of your parkour practice. The adrenaline comes from elegantly swinging and rolling through an urban jungle filled with everyday obstacles. The adventure comes from proving to yourself that such a thing is possible.

The Basics

If the fastest and most efficient way through a space includes clambering over walls, jumping across roofs, and running upside down while swinging from a bar, then so be it. That will be the path parkour wants you to follow.

Parkour is an outside discipline, with jams centered around "hotspots" packed with natural and manmade obstacles. Training includes standard strength and stamina builders, plus a heavy dose of learning to see your environment in a new way.

The most sure-fire way to become involved is by showing up at a parkour jam. Search online for a club near you.

THINGS TO KNOW

- × Parkour was developed in France by Raymond Belle and his son, David, in the late 1980s. The word *parkour* is from the French *parcours du combattant*, an obstacle-course training used by the French military.

- × Parkour is more about self-discipline than competition; the question "Who is the best at parkour?" is never meant to be asked.

- × Even so, marketers and sports brands understand the power of parkour and are cashing in on the movement. Cases in point: the MTV series *Ultimate Parkour Challenge* and the very existence of a competitive organization called the World Freerunning Parkour Federation (WFPF).

- × In response, parkour's elite now refuse to support or participate in events that undermine its noncompetitive nature.

- × Parkour's other problem, besides commercialization? People die, often in ways that spark outrage. Videos of fatal "parkour fails" litter sites such as YouTube.

TRUE OR FALSE? It is possible to run, unassisted and fully upside down, on a 360-degree loop-the-loop.

True. A British gymnast performed the feat in 2014. For his body weight, he calculated (correctly) that it's possible to run a full circle in a 10-foot-tall, 360-degree loop, by maintaining a constant speed of 8.6 miles per hour. It's harder than it sounds.

SURF AT MAVERICKS

WHAT Ride a monster wave, brah!
WHERE Half Moon Bay, California
BRAG FACTOR As big as the waves
LIKELIHOOD TO DIE Low (experienced big wave surfer) or
    Extremely High (everybody else)
BEST TIME TO GO November–March
PHYSICAL DIFFICULTY High
COST $

Surfing 80-foot waves on one of the world's most dangerous breaks?
It sounds suicidal to normal people.

To big-wave surfers, hit with a rush of adrenaline as they drop
into one of Mavericks' world-famous megawaves, it's why you surf.
It's what you live for.

Big-wave surfers get their chance at an annual event, officially
known as Titans of Mavericks, that takes place between November
and March a few miles offshore from the city of Half Moon Bay,
near San Francisco. Two dozen of the world's top big-wave riders
are invited each year. The conditions need to be just right (massive
swells and clear weather) and, once organizers send out the call,
contestants have just forty-eight hours to reach Half Moon Bay
before the start of the competition.

The Basics

If you're not invited to the annual Titans of Mavericks contest, you're kinda outta luck. It's possible to surf Mavericks whenever the swell is favorable (truly big waves happen only once or twice a year); just remember that even "small" waves at Mavericks can top 25 feet during a storm surge. Inexperienced surfers are not welcome.

THINGS TO KNOW

* Jeff Clark is the founder of Titans of Mavericks and a well-known big-wave surfer. Clark is credited with surfing the first big waves at Mavericks in 1975.

* Besides Jeff Clark, few people—certainly not big-wave riders—thought Mavericks existed or that California could produce any "big waves" worthy of the name. That changed in 1990 when *Surfer* magazine published a photo of Mavericks's monster waves. Later, in 1992, Mavericks landed on the cover of *Surfer*, and the surf world went berserk.

* Since 1999, Titans of Mavericks has hosted ten contests. The 2017 contest was canceled at the last-minute when sponsor Red Bull sued the event's organizers for breach of contract. The fate of the 2018 contest is not clear at the time of writing.

* Until 2017, women were not invited to surf in the one-day Titans of Mavericks contest. What's up with that, brah?

TRUE OR FALSE? Mavericks is named after a German Shepherd.

True. The dog accompanied the group of surfers who first rode a section of the now-famous break in 1967.

CIRCLE MONT BLANC

WHAT To finish is to win
WHERE Mont Blanc, the Alps
BRAG FACTOR Medium
LIKELIHOOD TO DIE Low
BEST TIME TO GO August
PHYSICAL DIFFICULTY Extreme
COST $

Run sleepless through the Alps by moonlight? Cross ten treacherous mountain passes in fog, rain, hail, or snow? Catch the sun rising, magnificently, over the glaciers of Mont Blanc?

It's called the Mont Blanc Ultramarathon (officially the Ultra-Trail du Mont Blanc, or UTMB), and many athletes consider it to be the world's most difficult and demanding foot race. On the trail, you are on your own. Just you and breathtaking mountain scenery.

You'll need more than one phrasebook on this high-mountain circuit. It crosses three international borders (France, Italy, Switzerland) and is the epitome of everything that is *alpine* in the Alps: towering granite mountains, glaciers, sheer cliff walls, and chalet-studded valleys.

The Basics

Mont Blanc's ultramarathon, the UTMB, is a single-stage course run annually in August, climbing and falling repeatedly, up and over 10,000 vertical feet through the Alps. The race begins and ends in Chamonix, Switzerland, starting at 6:30 P.M. and traces a 106-mile circle around the mighty mountain.

A maximum of 2,300 runners are allowed to run the UTMB. The fastest times clock in at 20 hours, though most runners finish in 25 to 35 hours (which means you're running over two consecutive nights without sleep!). The race cut-off is 46½ hours.

To qualify to enter the UTMB, you must complete at least three accredited long-distance races in the prior twelve months.

THINGS TO KNOW

* The first UTMB was run in 2003. That year, 770 runners started the race and a mere 67 finished. On average only 40 percent of runners complete the grueling UTMB (compared to the 95 percent of runners who typically finish a major urban marathon).

* British runner Lizzy Hawker is a five-time winner of the women's UTMB.

* Note: You do *not* run to the 15,781-foot summit of Mont Blanc on the UTMB. Leave that to the more than twenty thousand mountain climbers who annually ascend to the summit.

* Don't leave Mont Blanc without trying *genièvre*, or "Dutch gin," a juniper-flavored liqueur found only in the Alps.

TRUE OR FALSE? From a weight-loss perspective, running a full Mont Blanc Ultramarathon is equivalent to not eating twenty-seven McDonald's Big Macs.

True (if you're an adult male). The average male athlete running the UTMB will burn more than 14,000 calories, equivalent to about twenty-seven McDonald's Big Macs.

FLY A JET FIGHTER

WHAT Feel the need . . . the need for speed!
WHERE Nizhny Novgorod, Russia
BRAG FACTOR High (think: Tom Cruise in *Top Gun*)
LIKELIHOOD TO DIE Low
BEST TIME TO GO Year round
PHYSICAL DIFFICULTY Medium
COST $$$$–$$$$$

Cue the song "Take My Breath Away." Enter Goose and Iceman
flying F-14 jet fighters in loops and rolls at supersonic speeds. Cut
to Tom Cruise's inverted cockpit as he flashes the middle finger to a
hostile Russian MiG pilot while flying upside down . . . you've seen
this movie, right?

The 1986 film *Top Gun*, starring Tom Cruise and Val Kilmer as
ace Navy pilots, is an iconic bit of cinema responsible for an entire
generation's dream to fly jet fighters (and to look tough in leather
flight jackets).

You can legally fly a jet fighter in a dozen countries, typically
by sitting in the second cockpit seat of a two-person fighter such
as the Russian MiG-29, MiG-15, and L-39 or the American T-33 and
F-4. These are real jet fighters operating at combat speeds, performing loops, rolls, turns, and split-S maneuvers and pulling intense
g-forces (anywhere from 3 g to 6 gs!).

Can you fly at supersonic speeds? Yup, up to Mach two, which
is more than twice the speed of sound.

Can you fly to the edge of space? Yup, if you have the money to
spend. There's very little in the way of a jet-fighter experience that
money can't buy.

The Basics

Subsonic (slower than the speed of sound) flights are available at select airfields in the United States (Florida, New York, California) and Europe (England, France, Italy, Germany, Czech Republic, Russia, Ukraine). Expect to pay $2,500 or so for up to sixty minutes of flight time.

Russia is the only country where you can legally fly a jet fighter like the MiG-29 at supersonic (faster than sound) speeds. Most of these flights happen on a Russian military base in sprawling Nizhny Novgorod, a city about 250 miles east of Moscow. You'll pay up to $13,000 for the chance to hit Mach two while doing your best Tom Cruise impersonation.

THINGS TO KNOW

- The supersonic flights in Russia must be planned at least fifty days in advance. That's how long it takes the Russian military to perform a background check and approve your flight.

- You'll need to pass a medical test the day of your flight. The human body can handle g-forces up to 6 g for only a few seconds before you start to blackout and lose consciousness. Pressurized flight suits allow sustained g tolerance at levels up to 7.5 g.

- If the cost of supersonic flight is off-putting, and if you don't mind downsizing from a jet fighter to a propeller-powered fighter from the 1940s and '50s, try an air-to-air combat or acrobatic flight school. They offer one-day programs with much the same aerial thrills for less than $900.

TRUE OR FALSE? Only one *Top Gun* actor did not barf while shooting the film's jet-fighter scenes.

True. Tom Cruise and Val Kilmer definitely barfed. Same with Tom Skerritt. Only Anthony Edwards, the actor who played Goose, escaped without a single midair barf during filming.

SURVIVE THE SAHARA

WHAT Run the equivalent of five marathons in six days . . . in 120-degree heat

WHERE Ouarzazate, Morocco

BRAG FACTOR High (as in, 120 degrees Fahrenheit high)

LIKELIHOOD TO DIE Low

BEST TIME TO GO March–April

PHYSICAL DIFFICULTY Extreme

COST $$$$

The pitch sounds like it's from a bad horror movie: Run for six days through the endless dunes of the Sahara Desert, covering 156 miles in 120-degree heat with cracked, swollen feet. What fun (not)!

For long-distance runners, the Marathon Des Sable is the ultimate endurance race. The sand, the heat, the distance. Carrying all your own food and equipment on your back. Sleeping a few hours each night in communal Berber tents before starting all over again the next morning in the brutal heat.

The Basics

Each year in late March or early April, more than 1,400 entrants set off on the six-day, six-stage race. All participants dread the brutal final stage: a 50-mile slog through the desert.

Checkpoints along each stage offer water and medical care as needed. All participants stop to sleep each night in temporary campgrounds en route. The fastest time is just over seventy-two hours.

Most participants fly to Marrakech and then catch a bus to the village of Ouarzazate. It's a popular tourist hub with plenty of hotels and restaurants in Morocco's Sahara region. The race fee—about $4,500 per runner—includes bus transport between Ouarzazate and the Marathon Des Sables' start and end points.

THINGS TO KNOW

- ✗ Each year at the race starting line, AC/DC's song "Highway to Hell" blares over loudspeakers. No joke.

- ✗ The weight of your running pack can be no less than fourteen pounds and no heavier than thirty-three pounds. Excluding water, this bag is your lifeline, and it contains everything you need for the week: food, sleeping bag, and medical supplies (including a mandatory venom pump for snake bites).

- ✗ You are required to eat a minimum of two thousand calories per day. And yes, they check.

- ✗ For better or worse, there are no qualifying requirements to enter the Marathon Des Sables.

TRUE OR FALSE? The Sahara Desert is nearly the same size as the continental United States.

False. The Sahara Desert is actually larger than the US mainland. The former is roughly 3.5 million square miles, the latter is 3.1 million square miles.

Adventure Skill

HOW TO SURVIVE IN A DESERT

BASIC

Stay cool. Literally. Priority one is to seek shelter from the sun. Stumbling around looking for water will only make you sweat and increase your rate of dehydration.

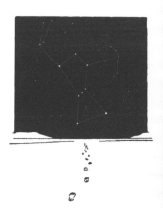

Don't worry about food. You can survive many days without it. It's far better not to waste precious body fluids hunting for sustenance in an extreme desert environment.

If you're stranded in a desert with a vehicle, do not leave it. Repeat: Do not leave it. Not only is a vehicle stocked with handy survival gear (mirrors, fuel for signal fires, etc.), it provides shade during the day and a warmer, safer place to sleep at night.

If you're stranded without a car, travel at night only and always in the same direction (use a constellation or star for navigation).

Find water. Look down and inside north-facing canyons or gullies (water flows downhill, and, in the northern hemisphere, the sun shines less on north-facing peaks). Also look for bugs and insects; they're often signs of a nearby waterhole.

ADVANCED

Every drop of water counts, so collect any dew that forms in the early morning, before the sun rises. Lay out jackets or tarps as dew collectors, if possible.

Do not drink from a cactus. It may work on television but, in real life, the water pooled inside most types of cacti is noxious and will make you vomit.

Don't bother with a solar still. It's another works-on-television concept that requires a plastic tarp and a lot of energy, with dubious rewards. If you have a plastic tarp, it will make a better insulating blanket at night and/or dew collector.

Do not drink urine. While urine is sterile and made mostly of water, urine is also full of waste filtered out by your kidneys. If you can urinate, you're not yet dehydrated. If you are dehydrated, your scarce urine will be highly concentrated with waste that will stress your kidneys and worsen dehydration.

Watch for dust storms. They can be deadly. If you sense a change in the weather or see a cloud of dust on the horizon, hunker down. Look for large boulders or low-lying outcrops for shelter. Also cover your eyes, mouth, and nose with a bandana or T-shirt.

Watch for predators. Mammals are less of a worry than poisonous spiders, snakes, and scorpions. Keep your shirt tucked into your pants, and your pants tucked into your socks. At night, sleep off the ground as much—and as high—as possible because body heat attracts the creepy crawlies.

RIDE THE WORLD'S STEEPEST ROLLER COASTER

WHAT Whhhheeeeeeeeeee!
WHERE Fujiyoshida, Japan
BRAG FACTOR Low
LIKELIHOOD TO DIE Low
BEST TIME TO GO Year-round
PHYSICAL DIFFICULTY Low
COST $

Never heard of Fuji-Q Highland?

Granted, it does not have the same cachet as Disneyland or Six Flags. Even so, this little-known theme park in the shadow of Japan's Mt. Fuji has one very serious claim to fame: It's home to Takabisha, the world's steepest roller coaster, opened in 2011 and certified by Guinness World Records.

How steep? A stunning 121-degree-beyond-vertical steep.

Think of it this way. You travel from 0 to 60 miles per hour in less than two seconds. Then you corkscrew twice, do a banana roll, are inverted seven times and then . . . it's the beyond-vertical stomach drop, with ear-splitting screams all around. At this point you may or may not need to barf.

The Basics

Fuji-Q is within easy reach of Tokyo, just two hours away by car or train. Tickets cost less than $50. While at the park, be sure to take a selfie with Mt. Fuji in the background. The views of Japan's most photogenic mountain are excellent.

THINGS TO KNOW

- ✖ The roller coaster includes more than 2 miles of steel track, but a ride takes just two terrifying minutes (112 seconds, to be exact).

- ✖ Fuji-Q Highland is no stranger to world records: Takabisha is the fourteenth Guinness-recognized record set by the theme park.

- ✖ Takabisha puts riders under a g-force of about four times gravity, similar to what fighter pilots experience in combat maneuvers. It's also the threshold at which humans can experience tunnel vision and temporary blackouts. Fun!

What is the world's fastest roller coaster?

Abu Dhabi's Formula Rossa, a roller coaster at Ferrari World that hits top speeds of 150 miles per hour.

TRY RODEO CLOWNING

WHAT The job is no joke
WHERE Branson, Missouri
BRAG FACTOR Medium
LIKELIHOOD TO DIE Low
BEST TIME TO GO Year-round
PHYSICAL DIFFICULTY Extreme
COST $–$$

Any rodeo clown will tell you the same thing: It's not *whether* you're going to get hurt, it's when and how bad. Getting kicked or horned is part of the job, even if you are fast and agile. Such is the life of a professional rodeo clown.

A key part of the job is protecting riders when they fall from a bucking bull. Step one is getting the bull's attention (wave, shout, jump up and down). Once you have the bull's undivided attention, step two is running away in a diagonal line. Bulls are faster than you, but their bodies are not designed to run diagonally at high speed. Step three is fleeing up and over the bull enclosure. Or, if that's not an option, jumping into your very own rubber escape barrel (professional clowns are required to provide their own escape barrels, so BYO!) and hope the bull loses interest.

The other part of the job? Be a clown. Keep the crowd amused. Make kids laugh. Juggle. Tell a joke. The best rodeo clowns both protect and amuse in equal measure.

The Basics

Youth rodeos are a good place to start: Many offer apprenticeships for aspiring rodeo clowns. Another option is enrolling in a professional rodeo school.

The Harvard/Yale/Stanford equivalent in the world of bull riding and rodeo training is Sankey Rodeo Schools, based in Branson, Missouri. It hosts no-experience-necessary classes for men and women.

These three-day training programs are just what you need to learn the basics of bull riding or rodeo clowning. Sankey classes are offered year-round and cost $400 to $600 per person (sleeping cot provided, grub not included). Sankey Rodeo Schools are offered at alternating locations in Colorado, Texas, Kansas, Georgia, Florida, and Wisconsin.

THINGS TO KNOW

- On day two of rodeo school, you'll graduate to practicing clown skills in a ring . . . with a riderless bull that weighs more than 1,200 pounds. The bull has horns and is always ornery. In other words, day two is the real deal.

- The annual earning potential of a full-time rodeo clown is about $50,000. That's assuming you can work eighty to one hundred rodeos per year and stay healthy (no broken bones or unexpected hospital stays).

- Nominated "Clown of the Year" in 2016 by the PRCA (Professional Rodeo Cowboys Association), Dale "Gizmo" McCracken is famous (as far as clowns go) and a long-term presence on the rodeo circuit. He'll also work your kid's birthday party for a small fee. Gizmo sells his own gospel CDs, too.

- According to COAI (Clowns of America International) there are eight commandments that all certified clowns must abide by, including: "I will learn to apply my makeup in a professional manner" (2nd Commandment) and "I will not drink alcoholic beverages prior to any clown appearances" (3rd Commandment).

What do you call an irrational fear of clowns?

Coulrophobia, after the Greek word for "stilt walker."

RUN WITH THE BULLS

WHAT Toro! Toro! Toro!
WHERE Pamplona, Spain
BRAG FACTOR Medium
LIKELIHOOD TO DIE Low
BEST TIME TO GO July
PHYSICAL DIFFICULTY Low (it's more about the mind game)
COST $

Running with bulls in Spain? In American pop culture, you can blame author Ernest Hemingway for making the idea cool. Hemingway ran with the bulls numerous times and wrote about it in his acclaimed 1926 novel, *The Sun Also Rises*. It's the reason why so many American college students consider running with the bulls a major rite of passage and something not to be missed, to the despair and worry of parents everywhere.

The annual festival in Pamplona, Spain, is held in honor of San Fermín, the patron saint of the surrounding Navarre region. Each morning during the festival, a half-dozen ornery, horned bulls are released onto Pamplona's cobblestone streets. Thousands of runners stand waiting, silently preparing themselves for the tumultuous wave of bulls and white-shirted people about to sweep past en route to the town's bullring.

It's an intense moment, hearing the angry bulls' hooves striking the cobblestones, knowing they're nearly upon you. In the following chaotic crush, it's a helter-skelter of trampling feet and shouts, with some people running up to the bulls and taunting them with rolled-up newspapers. And then it's over. You survived.

Running with the bulls is not for everyone. It requires cool nerves, quick reflexes, and a decent level of physical fitness.

Hangovers from the night before are acceptable, but drinking alcohol before or during the morning event is a major faux pas. You're running with deadly bulls, after all.

The Basics

Pamplona's Festival of San Fermín has been going strong for more than four hundred years. It's held annually from July 7 to July 14. The running of the bulls, officially known as the *Encierro*, takes place each morning starting at the stroke of eight.

Bulls are released from a corral in the town center and charge through streets blocked off with wooden barricades, for nearly a half mile to the bullring. It all lasts for no more than three or four minutes. Official *pastores*, bull "shepherds," follow the bulls along the entire route, keeping the animals moving in the right direction and ensuring that bull runners don't do anything too stupid or dangerous.

THINGS TO KNOW

- × The tradition of bull running was born out of necessity: how to transport bulls from outside of town into the bullring, where bullfights are hosted each day during the festival.

- × The Spanish fighting bull is known as *toro bravo*, a distinct breed selected for strength, aggression, and stamina. The ones in Pamplona inevitably have large and impressive horns.

- × Arrive early. The Encierro starts at 8 A.M. sharp, and would-be runners are turned away by police if it's too crowded.

- × There is no formal dress code, but runners typically wear white pants and white shirts, with red scarves tied around the waist and neck.

TRUE OR FALSE? No American citizen has ever died running with the bulls in Pamplona.

False. Matthew Tassio, a twenty-two-year-old from Illinois, was gored to death in 1995. At least fifteen people have been killed (and dozens of injured, usually from goring) since the festival began keeping track in 1910.

CONQUER TOUGH MUDDER

WHAT The more, the muddier
WHERE Multiple locations
BRAG FACTOR Low
LIKELIHOOD TO DIE Low
BEST TIME TO GO Year-round
PHYSICAL DIFFICULTY High
COST $

You've likely seen the Tough Mudder on television, thanks to multi-year broadcast deals with CBS Sports, the CW channel, and Britain's Sky Sports. It's also one of the world's fastest-growing athletic activities, regularly drawing a few thousand participants per event.

What's unique about Tough Mudder is teamwork. Unlike traditional endurance competitions, Tough Mudder is less about winning and much more about solving problems collectively, building camaraderie, and simply completing the event.

You crawl through the mud. You run for 10 to 12 miles. You face multiple obstacles that challenge you physically and mentally. You sweat. You may be in pain. You may cry. And you will find an unexpected fraternity of Tough Mudders willing to help you make it through the course. It sounds hokey and a little cultish, and it is. That's the genius of Tough Mudder.

Equally genius are some of the standard obstacles (events feature twenty or more obstacles, many unique to the venue): Funky

Monkey, a set of monkey bars slathered in peanut butter and mud, suspended over a pool of water; Arctic Enema, an ice-cold water tank you must swim through; and the Block Ness Monster, where you push, pull, and roll through 60 feet of rotating lubricated barriers.

The Basics

Dozens of Tough Mudder events are held annually in the United States and, increasingly, in Europe and Asia.

Whether you sign up solo or as a team, collective problem solving is part of the Tough Mudder ethos and you will end the day bonding with men and women who helped you, or whom you helped, to complete the course. There are few "lone wolves" when it comes to Tough Mudder.

Registration for standard events cost $150 to $200 per person.

THINGS TO KNOW

- The idea of Tough Mudder was a semifinalist at Harvard Business School's annual business plan contest. The cofounders took the idea public in 2010, hosting the very first Tough Mudder event at a ski resort in Pennsylvania. Nearly five thousand people signed up.

- Tough Mudder has an entire division of "obstacle innovators" whose job is to dream up and engineer new course obstacles. So yeah, there are people who came up with novel ideas such as the Augustus Gloop (think: climbing up a waterfall inside a mine shaft).

- If the full event seems too intense, try a Half Mudder (fewer obstacles, shorter run).

- Or, conversely, be a top finisher in a Toughest Mudder event to qualify for the prize money at the ultimate in muddery, the World's Toughest Mudder. This competitive event requires teams to complete as many circuits as possible around a five-mile course in twenty-four hours. Insane.

× People who complete a full Tough Mudder (nearly 75 percent of participants do) are known as "legionnaires" and become part of the Tough Mudder Legion. Some people have earned legionnaire status twenty-five or even fifty times. To date, one legionnaire has completed the event an astounding one hundred times.

What do the technology companies Yelp, Zynga, Angie's List, and Pandora have in common?

They were all founded, like Tough Mudder, by graduates of Harvard Business School.

BIKE THE DEATH ROAD

WHAT Quite literally, it's the most dangerous road on Earth
WHERE La Paz, Bolivia
BRAG FACTOR Medium
LIKELIHOOD TO DIE Medium
BEST TIME TO GO November–March
PHYSICAL DIFFICULTY Medium
COST $

In 1995, the Inter-American Development Bank dubbed the sixty-five-mile stretch of highway from La Paz to Coroico, in northeast Bolivia, as "the world's most dangerous road." Hairpin turns, sheer 2,000-foot drop-offs, fog in the rainy season, severe dust in the dry season, overloaded trucks taking blind corners at breakneck speeds . . .

The perfect setting for a downhill bike ride, no?

The road begins at an altitude of 15,260 feet on the outskirts of La Paz. Over the next 65 miles the highway—officially called the Yungas Road—leaves the dry, Altiplano plateau surrounding La Paz and descends more than 11,000 feet, passing through rocky mountain passes and lush rainforests.

It's largely a single-lane, rock-strewn track, often muddy and with few guardrails. An upgrade in 2006 addressed some of the road's dilapidated infrastructure and paved many sections, but make no mistake: In a bad year, more than two hundred people are killed traveling on Bolivia's Death Road.

The Basics

Most cyclists tackle a 35-mile stretch of road that is nearly all downhill, with just a few strenuous uphill sections, starting in La Cumbre and ending in or near Coroico. The first 12 miles are paved; the next stage for cyclists is uphill to the "Old Road," a highly scenic section untouched by the 2006 highway improvements. It's all downhill from there.

It takes about four hours to cycle between La Cumbre and Coroico, not including stops along the way to admire the hair-raising views. Bike operators in La Paz and Coroico offer guided rides ($30—$100 per person), which are highly recommended for safety reasons.

Cyclists ride the Death Road year-round, though the best time is probably the tail end of the rainy season (November–March), when the road is less likely to be washed out and before the dry season arrives with its heat, dust, and rock falls.

Whether you prefer a guided or DIY ride, it's best to start in La Paz, Bolivia's capital. Guided cycling treks typically depart La Paz in the early morning. Shuttle rides are an hour to La Cumbre, and you can take a bus back to La Paz in the evening.

THINGS TO KNOW

- × Unlike the rest of Bolivia, vehicles and cyclists traveling on the Death Road must drive on the left. Uphill drivers always have the right of way and forcing downhill traffic to the left (outside!) edge of the road gives more time and visibility to dodge oncoming uphill traffic. That's the idea, at least. In practice, it just means a lot of people temporarily driving on the unfamiliar side of the world's most dangerous road.

- × Since the late 1990s, the Death Road has become one of Bolivia's most famous tourist attractions, largely thanks to television shows such as the BBC's *World's Most Dangerous Roads* and History Channel's *Ice Road Truckers*, both of which filmed segments along the highway.

- × Bring cash in small denominations with you: The Municipality of Coroico charges a fee (less than $10) for cyclists approaching Coroico. The money is much needed and goes to maintain infrastructure along the highway.

TRUE OR FALSE? Bolivia is the only landlocked country in South America.

False. Bolivia and Paraguay are both landlocked.

ULTIMATE BUNGEE

WHAT The world's biggest, baddest bungee jump
WHERE Macau, China
BRAG FACTOR Medium
LIKELIHOOD TO DIE Low
BEST TIME TO GO Year-round
PHYSICAL DIFFICULTY Low
COST $–$$

Bungee jumping took the world by storm in the early 1980s. In the United States, you can pinpoint the exact moment: March 6, 1980. That's when the television show *That's Incredible!* broadcasted the first bungee jump in the United States. The jump was from Colorado's Royal Gorge Bridge, which happens to be the world's second-tallest suspension bridge, at a heart-stopping 1,053 feet above the canyon floor.

Television audiences were thrilled.

AJ Hackett was not involved with the sport's debut on *That's Incredible!* but he was a first-class entrepreneur. He recognized bungee jumping for its potential to become a mainstream adrenaline sport. He began to aggressively market the sport by setting a few bungee records himself (he earned a 1987 World Record for a jump off the Eiffel Tower) and opening the world's first commercial bungee jump operation near Queenstown, in his native New Zealand.

Fast-forward to 2001, when Hackett opened the world's highest commercial bungee jump, a terrifying 764-foot drop from Macau Tower in China. It's five seconds of adrenaline-fueled, stomach-churning freefall at speeds up to 125 miles per hour. It remains the tallest commercial bungee jump in the world, even today.

The Basics

You can jump night or day, in all types of weather, from Macau Tower thanks to its unique cable system (which prevents swinging into the tower itself, without affecting your speed of descent).

The cost for a single jump is $450, more if you include the optional video package (so you can repeatedly watch yourself screaming at the top of your lungs as you plummet earthward).

THINGS TO KNOW

- The first modern bungee jump is credited to members of Oxford University's Dangerous Sports Club. In 1979, they made a 250-foot jump from a suspension bridge in England (basing their concept on vine-jumping rituals practiced in the Pacific Island nation of Vanuatu). The jumpers survived and were immediately arrested by British police.

- The world's second-tallest commercial bungee jump (720 feet) is from the top of the Verzasca Dam near Locarno, Switzerland. You may recognize the dam from the opening scenes of the 1995 James Bond film, *GoldenEye*.

- Fancy a freefall jump from a helicopter into an active volcano? It's possible, though it's also more of a marketing stunt than a commercial enterprise. Volcano Bungee organizes six-day, five-night adventure packages in Chile that include whitewater rafting, jungle treks, a complimentary breakfast buffet—plus one 350-foot bungee jump from a helicopter into the steamy caldera of an active volcano. It's a one-of-a-kind experience if you're willing to spend $15,000.

Who were the three cohosts of *That's Incredible!*, the 1980s television show that broadcast the first bungee jump to American audiences?

John Davidson (actor, singer, serial TV game-show host), Fran Tarkenton (former NFL quarterback), and Cathy Lee Crosby (actress, played Wonder Woman before Lynda Carter).

DIVE OFF A CLIFF

WHAT It sounds like a fine idea, until you look down
WHERE Multiple locations
BRAG FACTOR Higher the dive, higher the brag factor
LIKELIHOOD TO DIE Medium
BEST TIME TO GO Year-round
PHYSICAL DIFFICULTY High
COST $

There's diving from a 20-foot cliff. Many of us have tried that. Then there is diving from an *85-foot* cliff, the way it's done by people like Colombia's Orlando Duque, a gold medalist in the nascent sport of high diving. He routinely jumps from terror-inducing heights of 85 feet or higher.

Cliff diving is a precision activity. You need to know the depth of the water, the exact height of the dive, the current tide, and how fast the wind is blowing. You need an intimate knowledge of the cliff itself and what lies below. When performing a dive over 90 or 100 feet, the slightest miscalculation can mean certain death.

Never one to miss a commercial opportunity, Red Bull now sponsors its own Cliff Diving World Series, featuring death-defying dives in six plunge-worthy locations including Ireland's Aran Islands, the Azores in Portugal, and Mostar in Bosnia and Herzegovina.

The Basics

Amateurs can dive wherever the water is deep enough, and the cliff height is manageable. Just keep in mind, when diving from 85 feet, your body experiences nine times the force of impact compared to jumping from an Olympics-sanctioned 32-foot (10 meter) platform.

You'll also be traveling close to 56 miles per hour and hitting the water with 4 to 5 gs, enough to cause a temporary blackout.

You'll probably be OK as long as you're diving into a minimum of 15 feet of water—and if the tide is not out! For cliffs higher than 30 feet, jump with soft-soled shoes on your feet and, once you hit the water, stretch out your legs and arms to slow your underwater plunge.

THINGS TO KNOW

* If cliff diving is a spectator-only sport for you, head to La Quebrada in Acapulco, Mexico. Five times each day, highly trained divers jump head first from the 115-foot-tall cliffs, into water that swells from 6 (deadly) to 15 (survivable) feet in depth. The swell is at maximum depth for just five seconds at a time; the jump takes three seconds, leaving almost no room for error.

* Amateurs craving a taste of cliff diving at manageable heights congregate in Negril, Jamaica. Locals—and more than a few tipsy foreigners—test their mettle jumping from 30-foot-plus cliffs adjacent to Rick's Cafe, a waterfront tourist magnet.

* The record for the world's highest dive is a strongly disputed 193 feet. What's not in dispute: Brazilian-born Laslo Schaller jumped from that height at Cascada del Salto, a towering cliff and waterfall-fed pool near the Swiss-Italian border. Schaller hit the water at an estimated 76 miles per hour and survived. The problem? You must meet two basic conditions to qualify

for a diving record: Exit the water under your own power and rotate your body 180 degrees from vertical. Schaller achieved the former but not the latter. Purists argue the world's highest dive remains the 172-foot jump by Rick Charls in 1983, while Schaller owns the record for highest cliff jump.

What do Elvis and cliff diving have in common?

The 1963 film Fun *in Acapulco. To earn the respect of a rival lifeguard, and to win the heart of a woman, Elvis jumps from the cliffs of La Quebrada. He nails the landing and sings the crowd-pleasing finale song "Vino, Dinero y Amor" (Wine, Money and Love).*

KAYAK VICTORIA FALLS

WHAT Ride the smoke that thunders
WHERE Livingstone, Zambia
BRAG FACTOR High
LIKELIHOOD TO DIE Low
BEST TIME TO GO August–December
PHYSICAL DIFFICULTY High
COST $–$$$

Kayakers inevitably argue about which is the best river in the world for an extreme whitewater adventure. However, few kayakers disagree that the Zambezi River, flowing along the border of Zambia and Zimbabwe, deserves a place of honor on any list.

The Zambezi is massive in every dimension. It's the fourth-longest river in Africa. In the rainy season, the river can flow as high as 150,000 cfs (cubic feet per second). This may not sound impressive, until you consider the fact that seasoned kayakers believe rivers to be running high at 5,000 to 7,000 cfs!

Just upstream from the main kayak run is thundering, towering Victoria Falls, one of Africa's most impressive natural wonders. Above Victoria Falls are miles of tranquil waters home to crocodiles and hippos; below lies infamous Batoka Gorge and some of the world's most sought-after Class IV and V big-water kayak runs.

The Basics

From July through February, the river is at low to medium volume, which is what you want: The cliffs become visible and the rapids are huge but manageable. The first eighteen rapids, covering about 15 river miles deep inside Batoka Gorge, are considered the best ones. The eighteenth rapid, nicknamed "Oblivion," is rated one of the hardest rapids in the world. *The world!*

DIY kayakers can catch lifts to and from the nearby city of Livingstone to the put-in and pull-out points for less than $50. Full-blown kayak expeditions, including camping and cooked meals, range anywhere from three to eight days for $1,500 to $3,000 per person.

Depending on your starting point, either fly directly to Victoria Falls on the Zimbabwean side; or from the Zambian side, fly to Lusaka and make the eight-hour bus ride to the city of Livingstone; or simply fly directly into Livingstone.

THINGS TO KNOW

- In 1855, explorer David Livingstone traveled down the Zambezi River by canoe to see the area locals called "the smoke that thunders." That's when he first encountered 360-foot-high Victoria Falls. Rising mists from the massive mile-wide falls can be seen 20 miles away on clear days.

- Devil's Toilet Bowl, Gnashing Jaws of Death, and Creamy White Buttocks are names of famous rapids along the

Zambezi. Only the hardiest souls attempt the ferocious rapid called Commercial Suicide. Walk around it.

✗ The Zambezi River is home to a population of bull sharks, which thrive in salt and fresh waters and are extremely aggressive hunters. Males measure up to 11 feet long. (Bummer. River sharks. Sigh.)

Who is credited with uttering the famous phrase, "Dr. Livingstone, I presume?"

Henry Stanley, sent in 1869 by the New York Herald newspaper to find Livingstone, who had not been heard of in more than six years. Two years later, in 1871, Stanley found a very sick and confused Livingstone living on the shores of Lake Tanganyika.

Adventure Skill

HOW TO SURVIVE A WATERFALL PLUNGE

BASIC

Don't fight the water. As it approaches the lip of a fall, water can be moving at more than 40 miles per hour.

Instead, use your precious final seconds to position your body correctly: face up, feet together and pointing downstream

Take a deep breath just before going over the edge.

Be prepared for bubbles and turbulence when you land. You will be temporarily disoriented. Don't panic.

Swim with the flow (away from the fall). Your body's natural buoyancy will help you to float.

The current is strongest immediately below the falls. So once you surface, swim downstream a ways before attempting to exit the water.

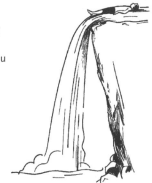

ADVANCED

As you're falling, wrap your arms around your head for protection, and cover your nose with the inside of your elbow. Close your eyes and mouth to keep water out.

Just before hitting the water, tighten your muscles to prevent catastrophic bone compression inside your body (shattered bones, punctured lungs, etc.).

As you hit the water, ensure your feet remain pointed and your body is vertically aligned. This will minimize the force of impact on your body.

Underwater debris is deadly. Cover your head as much as possible as you swim to the surface.

Cold water significantly decreases your risk of survival; the general rule of thumb is three minutes in water at or below freezing, up to fifteen minutes in water up to 40 degrees Fahrenheit.

PARAGLIDE WITH PREDATORS

WHAT Falconry meets paragliding
WHERE Pokhara, Nepal
BRAG FACTOR High
LIKELIHOOD TO DIE Low
BEST TIME TO GO October–April
PHYSICAL DIFFICULTY Low
COST $

Parahawking is falconry in flight, a hybrid of tandem paragliding and the art of using trained birds to guide paragliders to lift-producing pockets of thermal air. If it sounds crazy, it is!

The idea was hatched in 2001 by Scott Mason, who was paragliding around the world and fell in love with the scenery—and the wild raptors (in this case, Egyptian vultures)—found in the Himalayan foothills near the city of Pokhara, Nepal's so-called adventure capital.

His idea was beautifully simple: teach rescued raptors to fly alongside tandem paragliders. The trained birds guide paragliders to thermals and are rewarded midflight with a hunk of raw meat.

Best of all, two-person paragliding means an experienced pilot handles the flying and navigation, while passengers pay for the privilege of being the in-flight falconer, allowing the birds to land briefly on their outstretched arms to claim a tasty reward. Breathtaking mountain scenery, the thrill of paragliding, an up-close view of a mighty raptor in flight, and the knowledge that you're doing a small part to help conserve these majestic endangered creatures. It's the perfect all-around adventure experience.

The Basics

Paragliding is an adrenaline-fueled adventure in its own right. Unlike the rigid frame of a hang glider, paragliders are large, lightweight, wing-shaped airfoils with no internal structure. Pilots harness themselves in and make running jumps off cliffs or beaches or open fields, relying on air pressure to inflate the canopy and to provide lift.

The experience is simultaneously serene (aah, floating gently through the air) and terrifying (ack!, flying a few thousand feet in the air with no engine or safety net). Accomplished pilots can sail for hours on end, using updrafts to gain altitude and cover many miles of ground.

The parahawking experience costs less than $200 and includes thirty minutes of flight time with the birds. Flights are offered October through April, weather permitting.

Pokhara lies at the foot of Nepal's Annapurna region. It's a short flight or seven-hour bus ride from Kathmandu, Nepal's capital.

THINGS TO KNOW

×   In 2017, the Nepalese government temporarily shut down the Parahawking Project, due to pressure from animal activists who feared the unreleasable, rescued vultures were improperly treated (founder Scott Mason, a lifelong raptor activist, strongly disagrees).

×   In the meantime, until the Nepal project restarts, the Parahawking Project is offering tandem flights with raptors in Algodonales, Spain.

×   Peregrine falcons were the iconic bird used for centuries by land-based falconers in Europe. In 1970, with only thirty-nine pairs surviving in the wild in the United States, the peregrine falcon was added to the U.S. Endangered Species List. Using peregrines donated by hobbyist falconers, the Peregrine Fund oversees a breeding-and-release program that successfully rebuilds the wild populations. Fortunately, peregrine falcons were removed from the Endangered Species List in 1999.

✕ Mary, Queen of Scots, Russia's Catherine the Great, and England's Queen Elizabeth I were all avid falconers.

What is the fastest animal on Earth?

The peregrine falcon, which can briefly achieve speeds of more than 240 miles per hour.

TAKE A THRILL WALK

WHAT You're not afraid of heights, right?!
WHERE Birg, Switzerland
BRAG FACTOR Low
LIKELIHOOD TO DIE Low
BEST TIME TO GO Year-round
PHYSICAL DIFFICULTY Low
COST $

You have to love any adventure that begins in a walking-only village! It's called Mürren, and it's a tiny car-free outpost in the Swiss Alps. From here, a cable car ascends a few thousand feet to Birg station, which sits just below the 9,744-foot summit of mighty Schilthorn mountain.

The views are impressive. On clear days you can see all three of Switzerland's most famous peaks: Eiger (13,020 feet), Mönch (13,474 feet), and Jungfrau (13,642 feet).

However, that's not what draws thrill seekers. They come for the aptly named Thrill Walk, a 656-foot long walkway carved precariously into the side of the mountain. That doesn't sound too scary? Think again. The Thrill Walk does away with things like *floors* and *railings* (who needs those) and replaces them with open netting, glass-bottomed walkways, and all sorts of architectural trickery that make your heart race.

At times it feels like you're standing midair in a cloud, high above the Swiss countryside, surrounded by towering granite vistas. Just don't look down. No joke. Looking down is not recommended!

The Basics

The Schilthorn Thrill Walk, starting at an altitude of nearly 10,000 feet, is a steel path hammered into the vertical cliff below Birg station. Several sections require you to climb and crawl, including one daunting stretch of enclosed wire mesh creating an open-air tunnel that you crawl through. Spoiler alert: It's a looooooong waaaaaaay dooooooown!

Tickets are $85 round-trip for the Mürren-Birg cable car; the Thrill Walk is free once you make it to Birg. Afterward, head up to Schilthorn's panoramic 360-degree revolving restaurant, Piz Gloria.

Cable cars and trains connect the Swiss cities of Interlaken and Lauterbrunnen with the cable car in Mürren.

THINGS TO KNOW

× Piz Gloria is named after the secret hideout of James Bond's archnemesis, Blofeld. The production team for the 1969 Bond film, *On Her Majesty's Secret Service*, helped finance the first-of-its-kind revolving mountaintop restaurant and helicopter landing pad, both of which were featured in many scenes.

- ✕ Take the kids to see Schilthorn's Bond World 007 exhibit, with movie stills and entertaining descriptions of how Piz Gloria was built.

- ✕ Order a martini at the James Bond bar (shaken, of course, not stirred).

What actors play the roles of James Bond and Blofeld in the film *On Her Majesty's Secret Service*?

Bond is played by George Lazenby, Blofeld by Telly Savalas.

DEFY EARTH'S GRAVITY

WHAT To boldly go . . .
WHERE Las Vegas, San Francisco, Miami, Orlando
BRAG FACTOR High
LIKELIHOOD TO DIE Low
BEST TIME TO GO Year-Round
PHYSICAL DIFFICULTY High
COST $$$$$

As a kid, did you dream of being an astronaut? Is your fantasy to float weightless and experience life in zero gravity?

Lucky for you dreams do come true, as long as you can afford them . . . and can stomach the risk of barfing all over yourself, if or when you get airsick.

Space Adventures (the same company that organizes ten-day stays on the International Space Station—see chapter 1) offers eight full minutes of weightlessness aboard a modified Boeing 727 called G-Force One. You fly at roughly the same altitude as commercial airliners, achieving true weightlessness through the plane doing aerobatic maneuvers known as parabolas.

At the top of each arc you experience up to thirty seconds of zero gravity, floating freely inside the 727's modified cabin. You repeat the maneuver up to fifteen times, with the added bonus of experiencing both lunar gravity (17 percent of Earth's) and Martian gravity (38 percent of Earth's) before landing back on earth, wobbly legged and hopefully vomit-free.

The Basics

Besides being generally healthy, there are few limits to who can experience weightlessness. That said, it's not recommended for people who easily become airsick or seasick. To achieve zero gravity, the modified 727 flies level at around 24,000 feet before pulling up to forty-five degrees, introducing about 1.8 g on your body on the climb to 34,000 feet.

Pilots then enter a gentle 20-dgree dive that creates true zero-gravity conditions for up to thirty seconds.

Monthly scheduled departures are offered from Las Vegas (McCarran Airport), San Francisco (Moffett Federal Airfield), Orlando (Orlando Sanford International Airport), and Miami (Fort Lauderdale International Airport). The cost is around $5,000 per person.

THINGS TO KNOW

- ⨯ It's possible to have a weightless wedding. And if you depart from Las Vegas, it is possible to hire a floating Elvis to perform your vows. *Air Graceland*, anybody?

- ⨯ For a mere $165,000 you can charter the entire plane for you and up to thirty-three of your closest friends.

What is a "vomit comet"?

The nickname of NASA's original zero-gravity training aircraft, which first flew in 1957.

3

Adventures for Oddballs

*Strange and offbeat experiences
that scratch the itch of mystery.
These twenty-two adventures are
for the curious and open-minded.
You think, therefore you adventure.*

VISIT AREA 51

WHAT Earthlings, welcome!
WHERE Area 51, Nevada
BRAG FACTOR Low
LIKELIHOOD TO DIE Low
BEST TIME TO GO May–July
PHYSICAL DIFFICULTY Low
COST Free

The road to Area 51 snakes its way for miles across a barren desert landscape. It's quiet. It's isolated. It's eerie. And it's easy to see why this former top-secret military base has become synonymous with UFOs and conspiracy theories. Area 51 is a true mystery wrapped inside an extraterrestrial enigma.

For years, Area 51 did not officially exist. The U.S. government denied it had a top-secret military facility in the remote Nevada desert, 80 miles northwest of Las Vegas. The government also denied the existence of the U-2 spy plane, which was developed and tested at Area 51 in the 1950s and '60s. What, you saw weird lights flashing at night across the sky at supersonic speeds? Nope. Not here. You must be seeing things, the government suggested.

It was no surprise, then, that a suspicious public drew its own conclusions about the mysterious site. There are several hypotheses: Obviously, Area 51 is where crashed alien spacecrafts are sent for examination. Clearly, it's where alien pilots are sent for interrogation by the Feds. And most definitely, it's where the government is hiding its jackbooted thugs in black helicopters, readying to take away our constitutional rights, break in our doors, and seize our guns.

Oddly enough, many people who live in the shadow of Area 51 believe these rumors. The truth, they say, is out there.

The Basics

Area 51, hidden deep inside Nellis Air Force Base, is absolutely not open to the public. The Extraterrestrial Highway (State Route 375) runs along the northern border of Nellis, close to a salt flat known as Groom Lake and overlooking sections of Area 51. You can stop along the highway and do your best to photograph the low-lying buildings and hangars in the distance.

Another option is to make a beeline for the tiny outpost of Rachel, Nevada, and its infamous Little A'Le'Inn. It's a bar, grocery, and basic hotel rolled into one very odd meeting place for UFO hunters, conspiracy theorists, and bemused tourists stocking up on alien-themed T-shirts and bumper stickers.

The high desert is cold in winter and hot in summer. Tourists come year-round, but late spring and early fall are the best times to visit.

THINGS TO KNOW

- ✕ Area 51 was officially unmasked in 2013, thanks to declassified CIA documents that acknowledge the Nevada site was home to the United States' secret spy-plane program beginning in 1955. Coincidentally or not, that's the same time civilians started to report unidentified flying objects (UFOs) to local police.

- ✕ During the Cold War, the US government sent captured Soviet aircraft to Area 51 for study and combat testing. In the 1960s and early '70s, you might look up and see Soviet MiG aircraft in mock dogfights with US jet fighters.

- ✕ While no longer a secret, Area 51 and adjacent Groom Lake continue their role as testing grounds for covert military technologies. And business is booming! So much so that the government has a secret jet that transports construction workers directly from Las Vegas to Area 51 on a daily basis.

TRUE OR FALSE? Aliens exist.

True with 99.9999% accuracy. Given the universe is home to billions and billions of planets, it's mathematically inevitable that life exists beyond Earth. It's just not hidden at Area 51.

ROCK THE AIR GUITAR

WHAT For those about to rock . . .
WHERE Oulu, Finland
BRAG FACTOR Eleven
LIKELIHOOD TO DIE Only of embarrassment
BEST TIME TO GO August
PHYSICAL DIFFICULTY Medium
COST $$

Platform shoes? Check. Invisible six string? Check.

Laugh all you want, but air guitar is an ultracompetitive sport with its own world championships held annually in Finland since 1996. The purpose of the Air Guitar World Championships is to promote world peace. According to the event's founders, "wars would end, climate change stop and all bad things disappear, if all the people in the world played the Air Guitar."

Each August more than eight thousand fans gather in Oulu, in northern Finland, to watch competitors shred, solo, and power jam live on stage. To join the fun, you must enter and a win a qualifying event hosted by your local air guitar authority. US Air Guitar is the official association of the United States and organizes regional qualifying events for the annual World Championships.

The Basics

Individual competitors are scored on two one-minute performances, the first to a song of their choosing and the second to a random song selected on the spot. Real electric and acoustic guitars are allowed as props, as are over-the-top costumes and choreography.

Points are awarded in four categories: technical merit, mimesmanship, stage presence, and airness (a subjective category similar to presentation in figure skating—i.e., the amount of kick-ass airitude the competitor exudes).

In years past, winning songs included AC/DC's "Let There Be Rock," Van Halen's "Hot for Teacher," and The Romantics' "What I Like About You."

THINGS TO KNOW

- ✗ Currently Belgium, Bulgaria, Canada, France, Germany, Japan, Kazakhstan, Russia, the Netherlands, and the United States all have sanctioned air guitar associations and send competitors to the annual World Championships.

- ✗ Just don't do it: Air drumming or air synthesizing results in immediate disqualification at most serious air-guitar competitions.

- ✗ The 2011 gold medal was awarded to a woman for the first time (yes, boys, women play air guitar).

What did air guitarist Taryn Kapronica (a.k.a. Bettie B. Goode) lose on her way to winning the 2008 US Air Guitar regional competition in Brooklyn, New York?

Her toe. She jumped and landed hard on a metal chair during her performance of The Scorpions' "Rock You Like a Hurricane." Doctors later amputated the crushed toe.

PLAN A RADIOACTIVE HOLIDAY

WHAT Meet a nuclear babushka
WHERE Chernobyl, Ukraine
BRAG FACTOR High
LIKELIHOOD TO DIE Low (though likely to increase your odds of thyroid cancer)
BEST TIME TO GO Year-round
PHYSICAL DIFFICULTY Low
COST $

It's been more than thirty years since reactor 4 at Ukraine's Chernobyl Nuclear Power Plant exploded. It instantly became the world's worst nuclear accident, hurling radioactive debris high into the sky for nine straight days, blanketing parts of Ukraine and neighboring Belarus with deadly radioactive dust. More than ninety times the amount of radioactive material was released at Chernobyl compared to the 1945 Hiroshima bomb in Japan.

Since the 1986 accident, at least six thousand people living in the blast vicinity have died prematurely, mostly from cancers. The long-term health effects are unknown, but scientists blame an excess of twenty-seven thousand cancer deaths worldwide on Chernobyl's deadly fallout.

An exclusion zone with a nineteen-mile radius around Chernobyl was established immediately after the 1986 explosion. The zone exists today, but radiation levels are mostly safe enough to allow short visits.

Some tours include access to the so-called dead zone within a few hundred feet of reactor 4. Your guide's obligatory Geiger counter will beep and flash off the charts, but apparently, you'll absorb less radiation on a short visit to the dead zone than you will on international flights over the Atlantic. Go figure.

The Basics

A handful of tour operators organize day tours through Chernobyl's exclusion zone and the adjacent city of Pripyat, which once housed Chernobyl's nuclear workers and their families but today is an eerie, lifeless place with abandoned high-rise apartments and empty streets overgrown by trees.

The government tightly controls access to the exclusion zone. You pass through security checkpoints and have radiation levels measured both before and after you tour Chernobyl. All tours are preapproved with fairly rigid itineraries. That's probably a good thing, since plenty of radioactive hot spots remain in the exclusion zone. Stay on the path!

One-day and overnight tours depart regularly from Kiev and cost $150 to $200 per person. It takes an hour by car to reach Chernobyl's exclusion zone.

THINGS TO KNOW

- × Nearly fifty thousand people lived in Pripyat when Chernobyl's reactor 4 exploded (ironically during a safety test that went very, very wrong). It took the Soviet government nearly forty hours to order Pripyat's evacuation; most residents fled and never returned. Today, Pripyat's official population is zero.

- × That said, you may encounter humans living inside the exclusion zone. Don't panic, they are not nuclear zombies. They're known as "self-settlers," usually elderly babushkas who—despite all the dangers—refuse to leave.

- × It's not all doom and gloom at Chernobyl. The exclusion zone today is teaming with animal life: wild boars, voles, deer, elk, wolves, and even brown bears. If anything, large mammal populations are healthier inside the human-free exclusion zone than in many of Russia's official nature reserves.

TRUE OR FALSE? Episodes of *The Simpsons* with nuclear-disaster plots have been banned in Austria and Germany.

True. And in Switzerland, too! Apparently nuclear meltdowns are considered "unsuitable"—even in cartoons—in European countries trying to convince their citizens that nuclear power is a force for good.

Adventure Skill

HOW TO SURVIVE A NUCLEAR BLAST

BASIC

A nuclear explosion is preceded by a flash, which travels faster than the explosion's deadly pressure wave (winds up to 600 miles per hour). **Use these ten to fifteen seconds to seek shelter.**

Keep your mouth open to prevent your eardrums from bursting under the pressure. Assuming you survive the initial blast, *stay sheltered to avoid the highly radioactive ash and dust fallout.*

Wooden structures provide minimal protection from fallout. The best shelters are made of brick or concrete and have no windows (think basements in tall buildings).

Eat only canned or stored dried foods. Avoid eating plants or animals that may have been exposed to radiation (plants with edible roots, such as carrots and potatoes, are generally safe to eat).

Listen to the radio or television for news about what to do, where to go, and places to avoid.

ADVANCED

If you survive the initial blast, **you have fifteen to twenty minutes to gather supplies and find better shelter,** before the mushroom cloud's radioactive fallout hits the ground.

If you're unable to leave the fallout zone, do not leave the shelter for any reason in the first forty-eight hours. If possible, stay sheltered for nine days or until radiation levels outside drop to survivable levels.

You need roughly one gallon of water per day. Underground wells are generally safe. You can also drink water stored in heating tanks inside homes and office buildings. Water in plastic bottles is OK as long as the container is not punctured.

Wear gloves. Fallout will contaminate anything it touches, including you.

Geiger counters?
There's an app for that. Using a smartphone camera, apps for Apple and Google Android phones can calculate radiation levels in the environment. Actual Geiger counters are far more accurate. But hey, an app is better than nothing.

GO ZORBING

WHAT Unleash your inner hamster
WHERE Rotorua, New Zealand
BRAG FACTOR Low
LIKELIHOOD TO DIE Low
BEST TIME TO GO Year-round
PHYSICAL DIFFICULTY Medium
COST $

The idea behind zorbing is simple: Step inside an inflated double-walled plastic ball, strap yourself in, and roll. Downhill. At full speed.

Seriously, what could go wrong?

Zorbing was invented in New Zealand in the 1990s. Since then, it has earned a seat at the table of odd and extreme sports. Roll and bounce, hitting 30 miles per hour and hopefully not hitting anything else. It's fun, and maybe just what you need to shake things up in your life.

Zorbing comes in many flavors: tandem zorbs, competitive obstacle courses, hydrozorbing on water, zorb soccer, snow zorbing . . . there's really no limit to what you can do in a zorb ball.

The Basics

Rotorua, on New Zealand's South Island, is the home of zorbing and offers some of the most challenging and interesting courses to tackle in your roly-poly plastic ball. Rides cost as little as $30.

Full-blown "orb parks" (think amusement park minus all other amusements) have cropped up in Canada, the United Kingdom, and in the United States at places like Pennsylvania's Roundtop Mountain Resort and the Amesbury Sports Park in Massachusetts.

THINGS TO KNOW

- × Guinness World Records credits Steve Camp with the longest continuous roll in a zorb ball at 1,870 feet.

- × Zorbs made a brief appearance in the closing ceremonies of the 2010 Vancouver Winter Olympics, and they clearly caught the eye of the Russian Olympic committee. The zorb was an official part of the logo for the 2014 Winter Olympics in Sochi, Russia.

- × Zorbing's reputation took a hit in 2013 with a highly publicized accident. Zorbers at a Russian mountain resort rolled out of control and fatally crashed into trees and over rocks and finally onto a frozen lake.

What is the largest zorb ever made?

The so-called CarZorb, created by Nissan in 2014 as a publicity stunt to market the Versa Note hatchback. Nissan's CarZorb measured 60 feet in diameter and weighed over two thousand pounds (including the car, embedded inside). And yes, Nissan did roll it down a hill.

LEARN CHESSBOXING

WHAT Knight to e5 and left hook
WHERE London, England
BRAG FACTOR Medium
LIKELIHOOD TO DIE Low
BEST TIME TO GO Year-round
PHYSICAL DIFFICULTY Medium
COST $

The idea is wonderfully simple: Take the world's top fighting sport and combine it with the world's most competitive strategy game. That's right, boxing meets chess for eleven rounds in the ring.

Competitors alternate between three-minute rounds of speed chess and three-minute rounds of honest-to-goodness boxing. The first chessboxer to earn checkmate or a knockout, wins. It sounds thoroughly silly, but the sport has a passionate following and is taken seriously by participants.

The Basics

Chessboxing clubs exist in Germany, Russia, Italy, Spain, England, and the United States, many of which are sanctioned by the Berlin-based World Chess Boxing Organization (WCBO). Bouts are organized by both the WCBO and World ChessBoxing Association (WCBA).

Chessboxing is open to men and women of all ages. Frequent amateur nights mean it's possible to test your mettle on the board and in the ring. Join a chessboxing gym and train to become a pro (like Rocky Balboa, just a lot smarter).

THINGS TO KNOW

- × According to the WCBO, chessboxing was invented by Dutch performance artist Iepe Rubingh and the first match took place in Berlin in 2003.
- × Not so fast! According to the London-based WCBA, chessboxing was invented in 1978 by British amateur boxer James Robinson.
- × Boxer Mike Tyson fighting chess grandmaster Garry Kasparov? Nope, never gonna happen. Chessboxing uses weight classes and chess rankings (beginner up through internationally ranked) to ensure fair matchups across both disciplines.

What 1993 hip-hop song is the unofficial anthem of chessboxing?

Wu-Tang Clan's "Da Mystery of Chessboxin'," from the group's debut album. The song is an homage to the 1979 kung fu film, Mystery of Chessboxing. Extra credit if you know that Wu-Tang Clan member Ghostface Killah took his stage name from the film's villain.

VACATION IN A MICRONATION

WHAT Don't look for it on a map
WHERE Principality of Sealand
BRAG FACTOR High
LIKELIHOOD TO DIE Low
BEST TIME TO GO Year-round (invitation required)
PHYSICAL DIFFICULTY Low
COST $

First off, let's be clear what micronations are *not*.

Micronations are not microstates such as Liechtenstein, Vatican City, or Monaco—all of which are internationally recognized. Micronations are also not unrecognized states such as the Republic of China (a.k.a. Taiwan), the State of Palestine, or the Turkish Republic of Northern Cyprus—all of which operate as legitimate political entities but are not internationally recognized.

So what is a micronation? They are always small and always a bit wacky. Micronations may be governed by self-proclaimed kings or queens, artists, political exiles, or mutants from outer space. All you really need is the courage to stand up and proclaim, "This land is my land."

The Principality of Sealand is often called the world's smallest nation; it is housed in a World War II naval fort located off England's southeast coast. The fort has been occupied near-continuously since 1967 by Paddy Roy Bates's family and friends (Paddy himself died in 2013). Today Sealand is ruled by Paddy's son, Michael, the prince regent.

Bates originally took the fort from a band of pirate radio broadcasters and later declared it an independent nation. Interestingly, in 1968, an English court declared that Sealand is outside of Britain's territorial waters and not under British jurisdiction. Since then, more than 150,000 Sealand passports have been issued, despite the fact that no country officially recognizes Sealand.

The Basics

While Sealand's prince regent, Michael, currently lives in England, he and his advisors occasionally invite guests to visit Sealand. Bring your passport if you're lucky enough to score an invitation: Principality of Sealand passport stamps are often issued to foreign visitors.

THINGS TO KNOW

- You can apply for Sealand citizenship for 25 British pounds, which includes an official certificate and Sealand identity card (passports are no longer issued).

- Sealand also sells its own lifetime aristocratic titles including Lord, Lady, Count, and Countess of Sealand.

- If you are unable to visit Sealand, consider a visit to the Kingdom of Lovely. The runner-up name for this country was Kingdom of Home, which explains a lot. The country was founded in 2005 by Danny Wallace. He was the host of the BBC's documentary "How to Start Your Own Country." Wallace took his topic seriously and founded a country in the living room of his flat in East London. More than fifty-eight thousand people have registered online to become citizens of the Kingdom of Lovely. Wallace gained a fair bit of notoriety when he attempted to enter the 2006 Eurovision Song Contest with his heartfelt anthem, "Stop the Muggin', Start the Huggin'." His application was denied.

× Another micronation vacation option is the State of Sabotage. It has no defined territory. According to its founders—Robert Jelinek, H. R. Giger, and a 25-man screaming choir from Finland—the state may emerge anywhere, geographically. SoS is an art movement, music label, performance-art group, and secular-political collective that provokes thinking by intervening in the official discourse.

TRUE OR FALSE? Sealand has an official fencing team.

True. Strangely enough, the team is based at the University of California, Irvine. Sealand also has a soccer team, which played a charity match against England's Fulham Football Club in 2013 (Sealand lost five to seven).

JOIN THE FRENCH FOREIGN LEGION

WHAT March or die
WHERE France
BRAG FACTOR High
LIKELIHOOD TO DIE Medium
BEST TIME TO GO Year-round
PHYSICAL DIFFICULTY High
COST $

No fighting force in the world has deployed as frequently as Legionnaire fighters: in the past twenty-five years alone, Legionnaires have fought in Bosnia, Cambodia, Chad, Congo (both of them!), Djibouti, French Guiana, Gabon, Iraq, Ivory Coast, Kuwait, Rwanda, and Somalia.

In fact, the French Foreign Legion has been fighting near-continuously since the force was formed in the French colony of Algeria in 1831.

The Foreign Legion is unique in that it accepts most anybody; citizens of all countries are welcome, no French-language skills necessary. All you need is a passport and a ticket to France.

This loose acceptance criteria has long attracted men (women are not admitted) with questionable pasts. Fugitives from international law? Yup. Dishonorably discharged veterans from other countries who still crave battle? Most certainly. The force of roughly nine thousand is full of rough men with often dark pasts, willing to fight and die anywhere. And that's the way the French Foreign Legion likes it.

Since the majority of Legionnaires are not French citizens, earning a French passport is a key benefit of joining. You earn French citizenship after three years of service or after you've been wounded in battle, whichever comes first. This latter path to citizenship is known as *Français par le sang versé*, which basically means becoming French by spilling your own blood.

The Basics

You can join the French Foreign Legion assuming you are a reasonably healthy man between the ages of seventeen and forty and you have a valid passport (it doesn't matter from what country). There are no other requirements to join.

The Legion recruits in eleven locations in France. Show up and, if you pass basic mental and health tests, your five-year tour of duty starts immediately.

Training is brutal. New recruits undergo weeks of physical and psychological "hardening" at the infamous *La Ferme* (The Farm) training facility. There's also the rigorous *Marche Képi Blanc*, a two-day, 30-mile march in full gear, followed at the end of basic training by the seventy-five mile *Raid Marche*, another fully loaded march that must be completed in fewer than three days.

THINGS TO KNOW

- ✕ No French language skills? No problem, because daily language classes are mandatory. It's the only way to manage a force with nationals from more than one hundred and fifty countries.

- ✕ It's not a hat or a helmet or a beret. The legionnaire's distinctive white, circular cap with a visor is called a *képi* and you earn it in basic training after successfully completing the *Marche Képi Blanc*.

- Don't join the French Foreign Legion for the money. Your earning potential for the first two to four years (until you obtain the rank of corporal) is roughly $1,350 per month. On the plus side your food and accommodations are free. And this being a French outfit, your generous annual vacation is forty-five days per year.

- There has been just one woman admitted to the French Foreign Legion. Susan Travers, a British citizen, joined in 1943 at the height of World War II. She fought in North Africa against the wartime, Nazi-collaborating French government.

TRUE OR FALSE? American songwriter Cole Porter was a member of the French Foreign Legion.

True. The composer of such famous songs as "I Get a Kick Out of You" and "I've Got You Under My Skin" enlisted in World War I and served with the Legion in North Africa.

Adventure Skill

HOW TO ESCAPE
FROM A PRISON CAMP

BASIC

Stay healthy. Eat well and exercise. You must stay sharp to plan and execute an escape.

Volunteer for work duties in tailor shops, laundry, cooking, and other areas with access to tools.

No matter how you plan to escape, **acquire (and hide) basic tools** for digging (spoons, scrap metal), making disguises, and/or covering your tracks.

Bribe a guard. In exchange for money or love/sex, guards have been known to help plan and execute inmates' escapes.

Digging out is possible from cells made of brick or cement blocks. First chip away at the mortar of a single brick. Cover your tracks until you're ready to escape by refilling cracks with spit mixed with the removed mortar.

Make a dummy from sweatshirts or pillows and put it inside your bed. It's surprisingly effective in delaying discovery during overnight cell checks by guards.

Use a jacket or blanket to cover any barbed or razor wire fences that must be climbed.

Have a plan once you are outside the prison walls. Most attempts fail due to lack of preparation after the initial escape.

ADVANCED

Steal or make a guard uniform and walk out. This is bold, but often works on holidays and during events when prison guards may be paying less attention.

Fake illness. This may get you transferred to a less secure facility. Also consider escaping from whatever vehicle is used for transport.

Coordinate with somebody on the outside. While letters and visits (if allowed) will be monitored, it's helpful to have somebody coordinate a getaway car. Learn to speak in code.

If you're escaping on foot and likely to be pursued by human trackers, **walk backward in your tracks and leave confusing signals** (build a fire in the open, circle back repeatedly) to slow your trackers' progress.

Be prepared for worst-case scenarios. In some cases, death may preferable to being captured and returned to prison. Know what's right for you and have a plan.

DISCOVER A LOST CITY

WHAT Fear of snakes? Not a problem
WHERE Unknown and undiscovered
BRAG FACTOR Medium
LIKELIHOOD TO DIE Low
BEST TIME TO GO Year-round
PHYSICAL DIFFICULTY Low
COST Free

Are there any archaeological ruins left to discover in the twenty-first century? The answer is an emphatic yes.

It's true that the golden age of exploration has passed. Egyptian tombs and lost cities are harder to find nowadays. And, sure, there are no unmapped places left on Earth's surface thanks to satellites.

However, none of this is stopping archaeologist Sarah Parcak. She built an online platform to search the planet for hidden or lost tombs, pyramids, cities, and temples. So far, her techniques have located seventeen potential pyramids, more than three thousand ancient settlements, and more than one thousand potential lost tombs in Peru and Egypt. She's helping to protect these potential archaeological sites from looters and tomb raiders. The title of "Modern-Day Indiana Jones" fits her very well, minus the felt hat and bullwhip.

Anybody with an Internet connection can join the hunt as a citizen scientist. Maybe you'll be the one to uncover the next pharaoh's tomb or long-lost treasures from ancient Rome.

The Basics

Sarah Parcak developed an online system to crowdsource satellite imagery, leveraging the power of Internet users everywhere to examine small "tiles" of the Earth quickly, in search of potentially interesting archaeological sites.

The system was first applied to remote terrain in Peru. The results were solid enough to earn her a 2016 TED Prize; she reinvested the $1 million prize money into the recently launched GlobalXplorer° website. It works more like a game than a boring college tutorial. Start as a novice explorer, scanning four-square-mile "tiles" of Earth looking for signs of looting, then advance up the ranks. After five hundred tiles you become a Pathfinder; after five thousand tiles, a Voyager; all the way up to Space Archaeologist at fifty thousand tiles.

Parcak's team is notified once enough people identify the same potential targets. The method makes it possible to review the vast amount of satellite imagery available to archaeologists.

THINGS TO KNOW

- ✕ If you do find a forgotten tomb, you'll likely have no idea where it is. That information is kept confidential to protect sites from modern-day treasure hunters.

- ✕ To date, more than eleven million tiles have been reviewed by more than forty-five online explorers.

- ✕ In addition to revolutionizing the hunt for new or overlooked treasures, new technology is also being used to reexamine existing sites, such as the tomb of Egyptian pharaoh Tutankhamen. In 2015, a laser scan of the site revealed two hidden chambers overlooked by Howard Carter when he first excavated in the 1920s. Thanks to technology that didn't exist even ten years ago, the tomb of Egyptian queen Nefertiti may be found hiding in plain sight, just behind the burial chamber of Tutankhamen.

TRUE OR FALSE? There is no such thing as an accurate map.

True. Maps contain numerous biases and often distort geographic reality. It's why world maps using a traditional Mercator projection can show parallels and meridians as straight lines. However, in doing so, they misrepresent the shape and size of countries furthest from the equator. Africa is perceived as relatively small on most world maps when, in fact, it is large enough to cover China, the United States, and much of Europe.

RUN THE MAN VERSUS HORSE MARATHON

WHAT There are many easier ways to earn 500 British pounds
WHERE Llanwrtyd Wells, Wales
BRAG FACTOR Medium
LIKELIHOOD TO DIE Low
BEST TIME TO GO June
PHYSICAL DIFFICULTY High
COST $

Llanwrtyd Wells (the same Welsh town that hosts the annual Bog Snorkelling Championships—later in this chapter) hosts the internationally famous Man versus Horse Marathon annually in June. The race is run over 22 miles (just shy of an official marathon) and pits around three hundred cross-country runners against forty to fifty riders on horseback.

The original idea (fermented in a pub, of course) was to test the assumption that horses are faster than humans over long distances. The first race was run in 1980 and the horse won. It wasn't until 2004 that a human runner finally beat the horse.

The Basics

The starting line is located in the central square of the cute-as-a-button village of Llanwrtyd Wells. Runners typically start at 11 A.M.; fifteen minutes later, the horses and their riders are off (the staggered start minimizes injuries to beast and human at the congested starting line). A maximum of sixty horse-rider pairs compete in the race; there is no limit on the number of human runners.

For the fastest runners, it takes just over two hours to complete the 22-mile course.

There are no requirements when entering the foot race aside from an age limit (runners must be sixteen years or older), however entries are by lottery and fill up quickly.

THINGS TO KNOW

- ✖ Humans have the won the race just twice since 1980.
- ✖ Humans have numerous physical adaptations that enable us to stay cool while running long distances; we just sweat and keep going. Horses and most other quadrupeds, on the other hand, must slow down to cool down.
- ✖ So hope for a hot day if you are running: Warm temperatures are your key to outpacing a horse in a long-distance endurance race.

What's the longest name of any place on Earth?

Llanfairpwllgwyngyll in Wales, if that wasn't enough of a mouthful, the town's lesser-used official name is Llanfairpwllgwyngyllgogerychwyrndrobwllllantysiliogogogoch. Extra credit if you know the world's longest Internet domain is www.llanfairpwllgwyngyllgogerychwyrndrobwllllantysiliogogogochuchaf.org.uk

SKI IN THE DESERT

WHAT A winter wonderland at 106 degrees Fahrenheit
WHERE Dubai, United Arab Emirates
BRAG FACTOR Low
LIKELIHOOD TO DIE Low (certainly not from frostbite)
BEST TIME TO GO Year-round
PHYSICAL DIFFICULTY Low
COST $

Ski in Dubai . . . let *that* sink in for a moment.

Dubai is famous for its desert landscapes, riddled with sand dunes and camels. Summers are hot and humid, with daytime temperatures averaging 106 degrees Fahrenheit. So of course, it's the perfect place for hitting the ski slopes!

Ski Dubai, the Middle East's first indoor ski resort, is also the world's largest indoor snow park, appropriately housed in one of the world's largest shopping malls, the Mall of the Emirates. The superlatives don't stop there! Ski Dubai boasts the world's first indoor black diamond (advanced) run and owns the record for longest indoor ski run (more than 1,300 feet, with a 200-foot vertical drop).

There are tow ropes and a quad chairlift, toboggan hills, ice caves, and real live king penguins that make appearances throughout the day. If this all sounds hard to believe, welcome to the desert kingdom of Ski Dubai.

The Basics

The indoor ski resort opened in 2005, with five slopes of varying length and gradient from beginner to advanced. Beginners can hire instructors for private lessons, too. Snowboarders have a Freestyle Zone with jumps and rails.

The snow here is real, which means the temperature is kept at an appropriately chilly 30 degrees Fahrenheit. There's no need to pack ski pants on your trip to Dubai: Winter clothes and ski gear are included with admission. Two-hour passes start at $65 per person. Swimming (yes, swimming) with the resident king penguins will set you back an extra $350 per person.

THINGS TO KNOW

- ✕ It's a surreal experience wearing head-to-toe ski gear while ordering a hot chocolate at the midstation Avalanche Cafe. Just remember, it's probably 106 degrees Fahrenheit outside.

- ✕ Ski Dubai makes thirty tons of fresh snow each and every day in a space that covers more than three American football fields. It takes a lot of effort—and fresh, clean water—to maintain a ski resort in the desert.

- ✕ Tired of snow? Head over to the nearby Dubai Aquarium & Underwater Zoo. It's the world's largest indoor aquarium.

TRUE OR FALSE? The world's tallest building is in Dubai.

True. The Buj Khalifa is currently the world's tallest at 2,722 feet. It dwarfs previous record holders including Chicago's Willis Tower (1,729 feet) and Toronto's CN Tower (1,815 feet).

GO BOG SNORKELLING

WHAT Llanwrtyd Wells does it again
WHERE Llanwrtyd Wells, Wales
BRAG FACTOR Medium
LIKELIHOOD TO DIE Low
BEST TIME TO GO August
PHYSICAL DIFFICULTY Low
COST $

The idea is simple: Cut a trench 60 yards long, 4 feet wide, and 5 feet deep in a peat bog and force competitors wearing flippers, mask, and snorkel to complete two laps. Standard swimming strokes are not allowed; instead, competitors pull themselves along the bottom of the bog or use the doggy paddle. You think we're making this up, but we're not.

The World Bog Snorkeling Championship, first held in 1985, takes place annually in August near the Welsh village of Llanwrtyd Wells (yes, the same Llanwrtyd Wells that hosts the annual Man versus Horse Marathon).

The Basics

The cold, dark, murky waters of the Waen Rhydd peat bog is where the action can be found. Because traditional swimming strokes are not allowed, most competitors use brute force (running hard on their flippers) to essentially swim-run the course.

The competition is divided into classes for men, women, juniors (under age fourteen), locals, and novelty (costumes are allowed). Winning times are under two minutes, and hundreds of competitors come from as far away as Australia and South Africa. Online entries close seven days before the event and fill up months ahead of time. Don't panic: It's possible to enter in person on the day of the race.

THINGS TO KNOW

- ✖ It's a wetland bog, so hope for rain. The 1995 competition was canceled due to drought.

- ✖ Are you an experienced bog snorkeler who's looking your next challenge? Consider the annual Bog Triathlon. This event combines a one-lap bog snorkel with an eight-mile run and twelve-mile mountain bike ride. The Bog Triathlon happens the day before the traditional Bog Snorkel.

- ✖ Good news if you don't fancy a bog snorkel or bog triathlon: Food and drink, crafts, a bouncy castle, and live music are there to entertain the sport's hundreds of passionate fans and spectators. Llanwrtyd Wells knows how to throw a party!

- ✖ While bog snorkeling was invented at Llanwrtyd Wells, the sport has since spawned international competitions in countries such as Ireland, Sweden, and Australia. The current world record holder, Ireland's Paddy Lambe, completed a 2016 championship event in one minute and nineteen seconds.

TRUE OR FALSE? Peat bogs and marshes cover less than 3 percent of Earth's land surface, but contain twice as much carbon as all the world's forests combined.

True. It explains why governments in northern Europe are quickly moving to reduce the amount of peat harvested each year (peat is used for fuel and composting).

WATCH A CHUKKA
OF ELEPHANT POLO

WHAT An improbable, slow moving, and utterly mesmerizing
spectacle

WHERE Bangkok, Thailand

BRAG FACTOR Medium

LIKELIHOOD TO DIE Low

BEST TIME TO GO March

PHYSICAL DIFFICULTY Low

COST $

Thailand's capital, Bangkok, has many draws for travelers: ancient
temples, busy night markets, tempting food stalls, and, each year in
March, the King's Cup Elephant Polo Tournament.

Which is just the way it sounds, with polo played with six-ton
Asian elephants instead of the more traditional horses.

Elephant polo rules are nearly identical to standard polo.
Players attempt to knock a small ball into an opponent's goal using
mallets to strike and hit the ball. In the elephantine version of the
game, each team comprises no fewer than three elephants and six
players. Elephants are ridden by an experienced *mahout* or "driver,"
who acts like a horse jockey, guiding the elephant across the pitch;
and by a second player who wields a 10-foot-long mallet for striking
the ball. Games are divided into two "chukkas" or halves.

The King's Cup Polo Tournament is one of Thailand's largest
annual events in terms of attendance. That's largely because elephants, in Thai culture and history, are revered creatures and draw
huge crowds of curious onlookers.

Does the sport have a governing body? Yes, but of course. Meet
the World Elephant Polo Association (WEPA), which has a solid
reputation for prioritizing elephant welfare above all else. Proceeds

from all sanctioned matches go to elephant conservation programs across Southeast Asia.

The Basics

Elephant polo was the brainchild of two British expats living in Nepal in the early 1980s. They helped to establish the WEPA and the sport's governing rules. For many years, Nepal's Chitwan National Park was home to the annual World Elephant Polo Tournament between Nepal, Sri Lanka, India, and Thailand; the tournament hasn't been held since 2014 due to protests from animal-rights groups.

Thailand's King's Cup tournament, first played in 2001, is held most years on the Chao Phraya river in central Bangkok.

THINGS TO KNOW

- What's the most important rule in elephant polo? The rule forbidding elephants to lie down in front of the goal mouth. It's a clear foul and earns a free hit for the opposing team.

- What's the second-most important rule? The one about elephants not picking up the ball in their trunks during play.

- King's Cup elephants are always guided by, and rented from, local Thai mahouts. It's controversial, but mahouts are often forced to rent their elephants to logging camps or use them to beg on the streets. The polo tournament is an opportunity for mahouts to earn decent money and have their elephants examined by tournament veterinarians.

- That said, any sport involving elephants is unpopular with animal activists. Allegations of cruel treatment of polo elephants have led to match cancellations and sponsorship withdrawals. It also led Guinness World Records to remove all references to elephant polo starting in 2011.

TRUE OR FALSE? Elephant polo should never be played with soccer balls.

True. In the sport's early days, soccer balls were commonly used, until it became clear elephants enjoyed stomping on, and popping, soccer balls. Nowadays, hard, small polo balls are used.

BECOME A COMPETITIVE EATER

WHAT Dream. Dare. Eat.
WHERE Coney Island, New York
BRAG FACTOR Medium
LIKELIHOOD TO DIE Low (likelihood to barf: high)
BEST TIME TO GO July
PHYSICAL DIFFICULTY Medium
COST Free

It doesn't matter what kind of food it is, the goal of competitive eating contests is always the same: Eat as much as possible, as fast as possible.

Arguably, the most famous event in competitive eating is Nathan's Famous International Hot Dog Eating Contest, which is held annually on July 4th to celebrate American Independence Day. The event takes place at Nathan's original hot dog stand on Coney Island.

The goal, as ever, is to eat as many hot dogs (with bun!) in ten minutes as possible. The current world record is a staggering seventy-three hot dogs—one hot dog plus bun every 8.2 seconds!—held by multi-award-winning eater Joey Chestnut. The current women's record is 38½ hot dogs in ten minutes, set by Miki Sudo.

How do competitive eaters do it? The trick is to increase stomach capacity, because seventy-three hot dogs will simply not fit inside a normal human stomach. You can practice drinking water to stretch your stomach; you're in the zone if you can quaff a gallon of water in less than a minute. Just remember, no vomiting. It will disqualify you immediately from any serious eating competition.

The Basics

Nathan's hot dog contest is managed by Major League Eating (MLE), a quasi-official body that is all about marketing and corporate sponsorships. Only competitors sanctioned by MLE are allowed to participate in Nathan's contest.

To enter, you must win one of the regional qualifying events held across the United States. Eventually about twenty competitors make it to the main event on Coney Island, competing for personal pride and a share of the $50,000 cash prize.

THINGS TO KNOW

- × Officially, hot dogs are measured in units of one-eighth. It's up to the judge to determine how many eighths of a partial hot dog you've consumed. Keep in mind, hot dogs in the mouth when time is called still count, as long as you completely swallow.

- × It's no coincidence that antacid company Pepto-Bismol is a major sponsor of Major League Eating.

- × In the 1990s and early 2000s, Nathan's contest was dominated by Japanese contestants, including six-time champion Takeru Kobayashi. He introduced the so-called Solomon Method of splitting the hot dog in half, dipping the bun in water, and consuming it all at once. He also wiggles his body, ostensibly to force the hot dogs down his esophagus.

× Don't like hot dogs? No problem! Competitive eating events are held in dozens of categories: asparagus (record: 12 pounds 8 ounces in ten minutes by Joey Chestnut), chicken nuggets (record: 80 pieces in 5 minutes by Sonya Thomas), doughnuts (record: 49 glazed in 8 minutes by Eric Booker), and oysters (record: 47 dozen in 10 minutes by Sonya Thomas), to name but a few.

TRUE OR FALSE? ESPN's live broadcasts of Nathan's annual hot dog contest are viewed by at least 1.7 million households and generate an estimated $300 million in advertising revenue.

True. Competitive eating is big business.

RIDE YOUR BIKE NAKED

WHAT Bare as you dare
WHERE Portland, Oregon
BRAG FACTOR Medium
LIKELIHOOD TO DIE Low
BEST TIME TO GO June
PHYSICAL DIFFICULTY Low
COST $

The nonprofit organization World Naked Bike Ride (WNBR) believes indecent exposure to automobiles is the best way to defend the dignity of bikers.

Hmmm. OK!

More than seventy cities worldwide host WNBR-affiliated naked bike rides as protests for positive body image, for cycling safety, and against dependence on oil. The largest event by far is hosted each June in Portland, Oregon. Which makes sense, because Portland is weird *and* deeply infatuated with biking and bikes in all forms (tiny bikes, tall bikes, floating bikes, recumbent bikes . . . you name it, Portland rides it).

The 2015 Portland ride attracted more than ten thousand mostly buck-naked riders festooned with body art, plus the occasional funny hat. Keep in mind, this is a very naked bike ride. It's not a race. There are no prizes. It's not for prudes who can't handle the boisterous parade of genitalia cruising slowly down the residential streets of Portland.

The Basics

Portland's Naked Bike Ride is held in June and is free to enter. The race starts around 9 P.M. and the route is usually 4 or 5 miles in length over city streets.

Organizers and local police have an unofficial understanding: The ride dates are pre-announced, but the starting point and course are not. The former is publicized a week before the event, while the latter is kept under wraps until race day. All the secrecy is meant to minimize the numbers of riders and oglers.

If you want to join the fun, keep an eye out for the announcement (usually in February or March) of ride dates and get yourself, and a bike, to Portland. Pack light.

THINGS TO KNOW

- × Portland's Naked Bike Ride is part of a two-week annual festival called Pedalpalooza, which celebrates bikes and the people who ride them. Hundreds of bike-themed events and rides, live music, and parades are held throughout the city.

- × Do alcohol and naked bike riding mix? Kinda sorta. While it's not illegal to drink and ride, alcohol is not allowed at or around the starting point. Portland police do give tickets for intoxicated bike riding.

- × Not all Portlanders are thrilled when thousands of naked people cycle down their residential street. In 2008, a Naked Bike Ride participant was charged with indecent exposure and brought before a Portland judge. Not guilty! The judge ruled in the biker's favor on the grounds that naked biking has become an established tradition in Portland and is protected as a form of protest under the First Amendment of the Constitution.

TRUE OR FALSE? The current record for around-the-world biking is 123 days, 43 minutes.

True. The record was set in 2015 by a New Zealander who rode the required minimum distance of 18,000 miles and the total distance traveled (including flights, ferries, etc.) of 24,900 miles, which is equal to the Earth's circumference at the Equator.

WRITE A NOVEL IN THIRTY DAYS

WHAT No plot? No problem!
WHERE "Smack dab in the middle of your life," as they say
BRAG FACTOR Medium
LIKELIHOOD TO DIE Low (and only of ennui)
BEST TIME TO GO November
PHYSICAL DIFFICULTY Low
COST $

It happens at the stroke of midnight each November 1, when literally thousands of aspiring authors pen the very first word of their latest novel.

The annual kickoff of National Novel Writing Month, or NaNoWriMo, is something to either celebrate or dread, depending on the current state of your writer's block. You're ahead of the game if, by November 1, your book has a title and brief outline. Over the next thirty days (to be precise, by the 11:59 P.M. deadline on November 30) you have only one goal—to write 50,000 words.

No surprise, quantity counts more than quality. You "win" simply by completing a 50,000-word first draft, warts and all, in thirty days.

The only thing that matters is getting your ideas down on paper. You need to write 1,666 words a day to stay on pace. Don't overthink the plot. Don't overthink characters. Don't stress about dialog or—gasp!—rework and polish your novel's inevitably overwrought title.

Being a writer means *writing*. It needs to be a daily habit. NaNoWriMo exists to teach aspiring writers the invaluable habit of daily writing. You can revise and edit later.

The Basics

NaNoWriMo started in San Francisco and Oakland in 1999; the first year, twenty-one people participated. In 2015, more than three hundred fifty thousand people registered and more than forty thousand submitted manuscripts at or exceeding the 50,000-word minimum.

The world may not be ready for forty thousand quickly written novels a year, but hey, it's free to sign up and there's no doubt NaNoWriMo will make you a better writer, even if you don't hit 50,000 words.

THINGS TO KNOW

× Don't call it a novella. You're writing a novel, OK?!

× NaNoWriMo uses a 50,000-word target because they think it's doable, even if you have kids or a full-time job or are just plain lazy. It's also the rough word count of F. Scott Fitzgerald's *The Great Gatsby*.

× The first draft of *Water for Elephants*, Sara Gruen's award-winning novel (and later a Hollywood blockbuster starring Reese Witherspoon and Robert Pattinson), was written as part of NaNoWriMo.

Which is widely considered the first novel written in English: Sir Thomas Malory's *Le Morte d'Arthur* (1485), Daniel Defoe's *Robinson Crusoe* (1719), or Jonathan Swift's *Gulliver's Travels* (1726)?

Trick question. Scholars do not agree on the definition of a novel. All three are considered early examples of the format.

JOIN A CIRCUS

WHAT Unleash your human cannonball
WHERE Montreal, Canada
BRAG FACTOR High
LIKELIHOOD TO DIE Medium
BEST TIME TO GO Year-round
PHYSICAL DIFFICULTY High
COST $–$$$$$

It's the golden age of circuses, largely thanks to organizations such as Cirque du Soleil. Trained lions and elephants are on the way out, replaced by highly choreographed shows featuring acrobats, aerialists, trapezists, trampolinists, stilt walkers, unicyclists, jugglers, clowns, and performance artists.

Best of all, there aren't enough performers to keep all the circuses running! A worldwide shortage of talent means there's never been a better time to quit your job and join a circus. All you really need is dedication, courage, and a skill.

Dedication is for the lifestyle. Unless you're lucky enough to work for a so-called stationary circus (think a Cirque du Soleil show based in a Las Vegas casino), you must embrace a life on the road. You travel up to eleven months a year by bus, train, and truck, and sleep in campsites and cheap hotels.

Courage is for the physical demands. In the circus, your body is your career. The work is strenuous and often dangerous.

Skill is all about finding your passion and exercising it. You don't become a circus performer overnight. It takes dedication and practice.

The Basics

There are two time-honored ways to join a circus. First is to enroll in circus school. Circus Center in San Francisco, Cirque School in Los Angeles, Circus Juventas in St. Paul, and the New England Center for Circus Arts in Vermont offer workshops and classes for aspiring performers.

The prestigious National Circus School in Montreal, Canada, offers a Diploma of Collegial Studies in circus arts and, for non-Canadians, a Diploma of National Circus School Studies (DEE). Both three-year programs turn out some of the most talented, highly sought-after circus talent in the world. Yearly tuition is around $6,000.

The second option is simply to apply. Most circuses have job recruiters and a careers section on their website. You'll need a demo tape to show off your skills. And be ready for the in-person audition. Cirque du Soleil, for example, hosts auditions that can last two or three days.

THINGS TO KNOW

- × The good news: Many full-time circus jobs come with paid vacation, medical and dental insurance, and 401(k) retirement savings plans. The bad news: Circus salaries are not great. New recruits will be lucky to earn $30,000 per year.

- × There is no official age limit for performing in a circus. Just keep in mind that mainstream organizations such as Cirque du Soleil rarely hire performers older than thirty-five.

- × What is the most dangerous circus act? Statistically speaking, it's the human cannonball. Performers need trapeze-esque skills to gracefully fly 100 feet through the air, matched with the ability to stay calm and focused when stuffed deep inside a narrow, 20-foot-long, spring-loaded cannon.

× Circus fanboys? Yes, they exist. People (usually men) who obsess about circus life, specific performers, circus memorabilia, or circus history can join Circus Fans Association of America (CFA). If you can overlook the creepy stalker vibe, organizations like CFA are a wealth of circus information and schedules for circuses of all sizes.

When and where was the first Cirque du Soleil show performed?

In the small Quebec town of Gaspé in 1984. The show, called Le Grand Tour, was part of the 450th anniversary celebration of Canada's discovery by Jacques Cartier.

HAVE AN URBAN ADVENTURE

WHAT Obstacle course meets scavenger hunt meets bike race
WHERE South Bend, Indiana
BRAG FACTOR Low
LIKELIHOOD TO DIE Low
BEST TIME TO GO July
PHYSICAL DIFFICULTY Medium
COST $

Organizers call it a "scavenger hunt on steroids," but that hardly does it justice.

Started in 2009, the Urban Adventure Games has become the largest multidiscipline urban race in the United States. Think *The Amazing Race* meets a city-scale race connecting more than twenty-six urban checkpoints.

Two-person teams compete for the fastest times. The disciplines include running, biking, paddling, climbing, and office-chair rolling (there's usually a mystery discipline or two thrown in, for good measure).

The sprawling course covers the streets—and canals, police stations, office buildings, climbing walls, city pools, and obstacle courses!—of South Bend plus neighboring Mishawaka, including parts of the University of Notre Dame campus.

The event is legal, with full support from local businesses and city officials. This community spirit means race organizers are allowed to include some fairly nutty activities . . . like donning police body armor while handcuffed to your partner, and sprinting across a police-station parking lot.

The Basics

The race, usually held in July, starts at 8 A.M. That's when course maps are handed out to teams, which show each checkpoint and instructions for navigating between them. Checkpoints can be visited in any order, just don't forget any (or penalty time will be added to your total time).

You can enter in one of three divisions, from fun (beginner) to elite (get out of my way). While there is no designated course, the event is structured to take roughly four hours to complete. The fastest teams clock in just over three hours.

Running shoes, a bike, and a swimsuit are required. You will get wet. Registration costs about $150 per team.

THINGS TO KNOW

- ✖ Bring your own bike and—most critically—your own spare parts. Flat tires can ruin race day.
- ✖ South Bend's East Race Waterway, built in 1984, was the first artificial white-water course in North America. Spoiler alert: You will become intimately familiar with the East Race Waterway before the race is over.
- ✖ During the race, it is legal to ask strangers for directions and to spy on other teams. However, leave your cell phone at home—electronic devices of any type are not allowed.

TRUE OR FALSE? The University of Notre Dame's football team was once known as the "Catholics."

True, but slightly offensive. The university updated its nickname to the "Fighting Irish" in 1927.

WORK ON A FISHING BOAT

WHAT Born to fish, forced to work

WHERE Alaska

BRAG FACTOR High

LIKELIHOOD TO DIE Reasonably high (to be precise: 104 annual
   deaths per 100,000 workers)

BEST TIME TO GO April–July

PHYSICAL DIFFICULTY Extremely high

COST They pay *you*!

Looking for adventure? Need some quick money? Keen to spend a summer in the great outdoors?

Excellent. Then you're almost ready for a summertime job on an Alaskan fishing boat . . . as long as you can hack the long hours (thirty-day shifts with no time off), cold temperatures (it's freezing at night, even in summer), and cramped living quarters (this isn't a cruise ship, it's a commercial fishing vessel and you'll be sleeping tightly packed in cabins with two or three other deckhands).

From Bristol Bay in the far north to Ketchikan in southeast Alaska, the commercial season usually kicks off in April with herring and spring king salmon runs, hits peak season for salmon and cod in July, and closes off with king and dungeness crab runs in August and September.

You do not need previous commercial fishing experience to land a job on an Alaskan fishing boat. The trick is being in the right port, at the right time.

Alaska's Department of Fish and Game publishes an annual guide to commercial fishing seasons, which vary by species and location. Pick a port and arrive a week before one of the seasons opens. Your best bet is to walk boat to boat, asking for deckhand work. Pay rates are fairly standard, so don't worry too much about negotiating.

The Basics

Alaskan commercial vessels come in three varieties: trollers, purse seiners, and gillnetters.

Emphasizing quality over quantity, trollers drag stainless steel lines, each with a variety of lures and baited hooks, from a slow-moving boat.

Purse seiners lower massive nets to the seafloor and pull upwards of twenty thousand fish at a time.

Gillnetters (primarily for salmon) drop small nets in the path of migrating fish and entangle them by the gills.

Purse seining is the most lucrative option, especially for first timers; runs tend to be shorter, and crews tend to be larger, which translates into boats more willing to risk hiring inexperienced deckhands. Work on trollers is the most strenuous, with eighteen-hour days and no days off for a month at a time; as a result, the pay is excellent. On gillnetters, novice deckhands can expect to earn 5 percent of the total catch; you're pocketing up to 15 percent if you're experienced. If it all goes well, you could earn $40,000 or more during the roughly twenty-week summer fishing season.

THINGS TO KNOW

- ✕ In a bad fishing season, deckhands (even experienced ones) earn barely enough to pay for food and their portion of fuel for the boat. Unfortunately, there's not much you can do about a poor fishing season.

- ✕ On the other hand, fishing in Alaska is a year-round industry. It's possible to find work any time of year to offset a few bad months.

- ✕ Prepare for your new job by binge-watching episodes of the television show *Deadliest Catch*. It chronicles the lives of Alaskan crab fishermen. If you can't hack the show, you can't hack the job.

- ✕ The best way to remove fish smell from your hands and body? Vigorously rub fresh lemon juice—or toothpaste—on your hands and under your nails, rinse, and repeat.

TRUE OR FALSE? Timber cutting is the most dangerous job in the United States.

False. According to the U.S. Bureau of Labor Statistics, commercial fishing edges out timber cutting as the most lethal profession. Extra credit if you know drowning is the most common cause of death among commercial fisherman.

HOW TO SURVIVE FALLING OVERBOARD AT SEA

BASIC

From taller passenger and cargo ships, enter the water feet first to minimize broken bones and head injuries.

In cold waters, especially, take a deep breath before impact. You are at risk of swallowing sea water and drowning if your lungs are not already filled with air. Involuntary gasping is the body's shock response when the temperature of your skin drops abruptly.

Do not thrash or swim with outstretched arms (it cools the body). Conserve your heat and energy by staying as still as possible. Float if you can.

Keep a positive mental attitude and do not give up.

Even in 40-degree (Fahrenheit) waters, hypothermia in is not a major risk for fifteen to thirty minutes. This is the amount of time rescuers have to find and extract you.

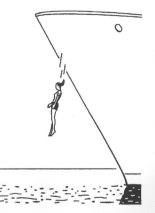

ADVANCED

Risk factors for commercial fishermen include rough seas, slick decks, and being entangled in fishing gear. Wearing flotation devices dramatically increases your odds of survival.

Commercial fisherman can use rubber boots as improvised flotation devices. Remove and fill the boots with air, hold them under your arms, and float or gently tread water.

Do not relax as rescuers approach. More than 20 percent of fatalities occur during the rescue phase due to the effects of cold incapacitation (the inability to coordinate movement needed for swimming or grabbing a life ring or rescue ladder).

If you lose sight of your ship and can see shore of any kind, swim toward it.

VOLUNTEER AS A FIRE SPOTTER

WHAT Only you can prevent forest fires
WHERE US national forests
BRAG FACTOR Medium
LIKELIHOOD TO DIE Low
BEST TIME TO GO April–September
PHYSICAL DIFFICULTY Low
COST $

Like milkman and chimney sweep, the job of fire spotter seems mildly old fashioned.

And yet, each year, the US Forest Service advertises dozens of fire-spotting roles in national forests across the country. In a nod to modernity, the role is nowadays known as "forestry technician," but don't be fooled. Your job is the same as it ever was, to scan the horizons for smoke.

The job is straightforward: From 9 A.M. to 5 P.M. each day, you look for smoke (binoculars are handy) and estimate its azimuth, distance, and location, as well as its volume and color. All of this helps the Forest Service determine if and when to call out the firefighters, in case of a major conflagration.

The real adventure is your commute: Typically, you'll walk a few steps from your tent and campfire, then climb a few score stairs to the top of your private viewing platform. The 360-degree views over the sprawling forest are, by far, the best part of your job.

The Basics

Fire spotters serve an important role and the Forest Service doesn't hire just anybody. There's an application process and, if you're selected, some basic training required. You also need a high school degree plus two years of college, community college, or similar educational experience.

The nonprofit Forest Fire Lookout Association (FFLA) maintains an extensive list of fire-spotting jobs. While some fire-spotting roles are paid, the majority are volunteer. Depending on location, positions last continuously from late winter and early spring through early autumn.

Sometimes you're allowed guests in the fire towers, sometimes not. In truly remote locations, you may have little company beyond animals and the occasional backpacker.

THINGS TO KNOW

* While many fire spotters work as unpaid volunteers, some positions are paid, anywhere from $13 to $17 per hour. Even then, fire spotting is not really a career, so much as a paid summertime adventure.

* Fires on public forestry lands were once feared and, as a result, aggressively suppressed by the government—hence the network of more than 1,500 fire lookouts maintained in the United States.

* More recently, the Forest Service has recognized the benefits of fire to forest ecosystems and is increasingly lenient about allowing certain lightning-caused burns to roam unmolested.

* Although large sections of national forest are consumed each year by fire, spotters can go weeks at a time without seeing a hint of smoke. During these lulls you'll want a good book to read, an axe to chop firewood, and maybe a creative hobby. Fire spotters are often aspiring poets, playwrights, and painters.

Adventure Skill

HOW TO SURVIVE
A FOREST FIRE

BASIC

If you can safely leave the area around a wildfire, do so. Evacuation is always preferable to sheltering in place.

Always move away and upwind (into the wind) from a fire. Look up and observe which way the smoke is blowing. Move in the opposite direction.

Always retreat downhill from a wildfire. Flames travel uphill, along with deadly superheated air created by the fire.

As you move upwind and downhill, search for natural firebreaks such as a road, river, lake, or clear-cut area of trees. The less combustible material around you, the better.

ADVANCED

Do not cover your mouth with a wet bandana or cloth. Neither material is fine enough to filter out smoke particles. And any moisture is likely to boil and blister your skin.

Don't try to outrun a wildfire. A wall of flame can move at 30 to 40 miles per hour and easily overtake you.

If you must run, head toward streams or low areas. Run through the leading edge of a fire into areas that have already burned as a last resort.

If flames are upon you, take a deep breath and hold it. Inhaling superheated air will kill you. Seek cover in a ditch or any low ground to allow superheated air to pass overhead.

Worst-case: dig in. Cut a trench in low ground and lie with your feet facing the direction of the fire. Cover yourself with dirt and wait for the fire to pass over.

TRUE OR FALSE? Novelist Jack Kerouac was a paid fire spotter.

True. In the early 1950s, Kerouac spent two months in Washington State's Desolation Wilderness as a fire lookout. He wrote about the experience in his books Lonesome Traveler and The Dharma Bums.

FAKE YOUR OWN KIDNAPPING

WHAT The perfect gift for hard-to-shop-for friends
WHERE An anonymous basement
BRAG FACTOR High
LIKELIHOOD TO DIE Low
BEST TIME TO GO Dead of night
PHYSICAL DIFFICULTY High
COST $$–$$$

Some people dream of relaxing beach vacations. Others dream of being forcibly abducted. Perhaps getting kidnapped is just the thing for your next weekend getaway.

The concept is controversial. Fake kidnappings are not every-body's proverbial cup of tea. Even so, companies in the United States and Europe offer a variety of kidnapping packages. So-called first kidnappings include forced abduction from a public location (a supermarket parking lot, usually), being handcuffed and gagged, and then locked away in a basement where you will be subject to the stress and psychological pressures of a real-life kidnapping for up to four hours.

Ten-hour "real kidnappings" that can be customized to include ransom notes and physical abuse such as waterboarding, being duct-taped to a wall, suspended from a ceiling, stuffed into a closet, hit by a stun gun, beaten with a dead fish . . . there's literally no limit to what money can buy when it comes to fake-your-own kidnap-ping scenarios.

The Basics

A handful of companies legally provide fake kidnapping "entertain-ment" services. The process generally starts with a questionnaire probing your tolerance of various physical and mental stressors, your allergies, and any preexisting medical conditions. Most also ask for a safe word that, if spoken, immediately ends the kidnap-ping. You may also agree on a backstory to give your kidnapping a narrative arc.

First-timers pay $500 to $700 and generally travel to their kidnapper's location, check into a cheap hotel, and wait for the kidnappers to make their move. You'll be taken to a secure location and tied up, mentally abused, and possibly physically tortured. After four hours, you're released and dropped back at your hotel.

More advanced scenarios—as in, more realistic—last ten hours or more and cost upwards of $1,500.

THINGS TO KNOW

- ✕ Extreme Kidnapping, run by counterfeiter and ex-convict Adam Thicke, was the first US company to organize fake kidnappings for a fee. Thicke no longer kidnaps the general public; he's moved on to the more lucrative kidnapping-as-corporate-team-building market.

- ✕ The worst part of being kidnapped? According to a *GQ* journalist abducted by Extreme Kidnapping, it was being forced to listen to The Eurythmics' song "Sweet Dreams" over and over and over and over again.

- ✕ Is fake kidnapping legal? Mostly, yes. You can fake a kidnapping in the United States as long as it doesn't cause the police to be called or a police report to be filed, and as long as your kidnappers don't actually defraud you or shake you down for money (not counting the "entertainment fee" you've already paid).

- ✕ Craving something more than a basic kidnapping? Ultime Réalité, a Paris-based "reality adventure" company, offers kidnapping by gunpoint, man-hunting (tracking humans in urban or jungle settings), overnights at a morgue, and "Go Fast" adventures that include transporting and unloading fake drugs off a helicopter or speedboat in the dead of night.

What body part did the kidnappers of sixteen-year-old John Paul Getty III, son of the world's richest man at the time, cut off and send as proof of life and a sign they were deadly serious about collecting a $17 million ransom?

His ear. Getty's father originally balked at paying any ransom for his estranged son. Three months after Getty was abducted, the kidnappers sent his severed ear to an Italian newspaper. The ransom was negotiated down to $3 million and paid.

Adventure Skill

HOW TO EVADE A KIDNAPPING ATTEMPT

BASIC

Some kidnappers patrol wealthy areas and look for easy, obvious targets. Blend in. Do not wear flashy jewelry or carry an expensive camera or video gear. Do not use street-facing ATMs.

If you're driving, keep doors locked and windows rolled up. Don't give kidnappers an opportunity to enter your vehicle.

When not driving, use public transit or hotel shuttles, or walk. You're most vulnerable in a taxi.

Actively resist. Assume the worst and do everything possible—bite, kick, scream—to draw attention and thwart your abductors. Fight dirty.

If you're physically overwhelmed or in a life-threatening situation, appear to surrender and reserve your strength. Stay calm, and look for the first opportunity to escape.

ADVANCED

Always leave an entire car length between you and the vehicle directly ahead, especially in heavy traffic and at traffic signals. If kidnappers attempt to box you in, you'll have some room to maneuver and potentially flee.

Carry a dummy wallet with just one credit card and limited cash in an obvious pocket or purse. Hide the bulk of your cash and credit cards, and your passport, in your hotel or on your body.

If you sense danger approaching, call 911 or the equivalent and hide the phone on your body (if possible) and prepare to fight.
Use your keys as an improvised weapon by inserting them between your fingers to slash an attacker's face and eyes.

If your abductor uses restraints, actively present your hands in front of your body (instead of behind your back).
Spread your fingers and legs to create slack in your restraints.

If abducted and placed into a vehicle, pay attention to what direction you're moving and any landmarks you can identify. If you're blindfolded, listen for trains, rivers, factories, or other loud distinct sounds that may indicate your location.

RACE A RICKSHAW ACROSS INDIA

WHAT The least sensible thing you can do with two weeks
WHERE Jaisalmer to Kochi, India
BRAG FACTOR High
LIKELIHOOD TO DIE Medium
BEST TIME TO GO January, April, or August
PHYSICAL DIFFICULTY High
COST $$$–$$$$

The infamous Rickshaw Run has a starting line and, roughly 1,800 miles away, a finish line—and nothing else in between.

There is no official route. There are no pit stops or check-ins or race requirements other than driving your rickshaw from Jaisalmer in northern India to Kochi in southern India.

This isn't a race in the traditional sense. Think of it more like the oddest way possible to experience the wonders of India, all from a slow-moving motorized rickshaw rattling and bumping and stalling out and spewing fumes on potholed roads overrun by cows, buses, motorbikes, and trucks.

For some people, the experience is hell on earth; for others, it's the most fun you can possibly have on three wheels.

The hosts of Rickshaw Run call it an "un-race" since, really, anybody traveling the length of India by rickshaw is not going anywhere fast. Rickshaw Runs are held two or three times annually and last from two to three weeks (normal people in normal cars cover the same distance in about four days; on express trains the same journey lasts two days).

The Basics

Entrance fees (up to a maximum of three people) are $2,100 and include use of your very own two-cylinder, single-stroke auto rickshaw for the duration of the race.

Races start with a mandatory two days of test driving and rickshaw familiarization; over the course of two weeks it's guaranteed your rickshaw will break down, puncture a tire, tip over and so forth, so it's wise to know how to make modest repairs on the go.

Insurance is included in the race fee. The only other money you need is for food, lodging, spare parts, fuel, and bribes for Indian police officers uncomfortable with the idea of you driving a rickshaw from Jaisalmer to Kochi without a little something for their troubles. Another $2,000 or so should cover your expenses.

THINGS TO KNOW

- ✕ Motorized rickshaws have been around since the 1930s. The iconic model produced by Indian company Bajaj—the same model used in Rickshaw Runs—was invented in 1947 by Italian aerospace engineer Corradino D'Ascanio.

- ✕ D'Ascanio's other claim to fame? He invented the Vespa motor scooter.

- ✕ More than eighty-five rickshaw teams complete each Jaisalmer to Kochi circuit, and space is limited. To join the fun, you'll need to sign up at least six months in advance.

- ✕ Prepare for your race by watching the 2007 film *Amal*, about a humble rickshaw driver from New Delhi.

What is the top recommended speed of a Bajaj auto rickshaw, according to its manufacturer?

Roughly 35 miles per hour (presumably a bit faster on the downhill).

START A TOMATO FIGHT

WHAT Twenty-five thousand people, so many tomatoes
WHERE Buñol, Spain
BRAG FACTOR Soggy
LIKELIHOOD TO DIE Low
BEST TIME TO GO August
PHYSICAL DIFFICULTY Low
COST $

It's billed as the world's largest food fight. Each August, more than twenty-five thousand people descend on the Spanish town of Buñol to celebrate the festival of La Tomatina. The idea is beautifully simple. The entire city throws tomatoes at each other, more than three hundred thousand pounds of tomatoes, nonstop, for a full hour.

Tomatoes in the face, tomatoes in your hair, tomatoes down the back of your shirt, tomatoes in your shoes . . .

When it's over, the streets of Buñol are deeply permeated with tomatoes in various stages of disintegration, from smooshed and smashed to crushed, pasted, and fully sauced. Eventually the town's fire department rolls out the hoses for a much needed, city-wide deep cleaning.

La Tomatina is one of those rare festivals that happens without a reason. It's not a religious event. It does not commemorate a poignant moment in Spanish history or mark a day of cultural significance. Locals think the first tomatoes were thrown in the 1940s but, then again, nobody really knows.

The Basics

La Tomatina is held annually on the last Wednesday in August. The city hosts parades and fireworks in the week leading up to the tomato fight; massive quantities of overripe tomatoes are trucked into the city from across southeastern Spain.

On the morning of the big battle, a ham is placed atop a tall greased pole (the Palo Jabón) and La Tomatina officially starts once someone clambers to the top and knocks the ham down. The next sixty minutes are a chaotic blur of mushy tomatoes flying in every direction. Wearing goggles and gloves is highly recommended. And at the risk of stating the obvious, every part of you will end up soaked in sticky tomato goo. Ditch the fancy clothes and expensive shoes.

Because of the large crowds, tickets are now required to enter the city on the day of the event; they can (and should) be prepurchased online for a small fee. Buñol is a small city and cannot accommodate the massive crowds who arrive for La Tomatina. Book a room far in advance or, even better, sleep in nearby Valencia and bus into Buñol along with thousands of fellow tomato throwers.

THINGS TO KNOW

- × La Tomatina is not BYOT (bring your own tomatoes). To avoid injuries, organizers only allow overripe tomatoes that have been presquashed. All other tomatoes will be confiscated!

- × La Tomatina has had a rocky history; during Spain's totalitarian era under dictator Francisco Franco, the event was canceled numerous times by city leaders who were concerned that the city-wide tomato fight could easily turn into a city-wide political protest. Unpopular dictators are understandably wary of festivals involving rotten tomatoes.

✖ Tomatoes are, scientifically speaking, definitely not vegetables. Like all true fruits, tomatoes contain the seeds of the plant, like blueberries and oranges. The vegetable-or-fruit confusion likely stems from the fact that tomatoes are typically cooked in savory dishes and rarely served in sweet dishes.

TRUE OR FALSE? Tomatoes are poisonous to dogs.

Mostly true. Young green tomatoes, tomato plants, and stems have high concentrations of tomatine, which can kill dogs if eaten in large quantities. Ripe tomatoes are generally considered safe for dogs.

4

Adventures for Mind, Body, and Spirit

Get self-actualized—or get lost. These twenty-two adventures are for people seeking a few thrills on the road to self-discovery and enlightenment.

SEND A NOTE TO GOD

WHAT Sent from Western Wall. Please excuse any typos.
WHERE Jerusalem, Israel
BRAG FACTOR For observant Jews, it's the holiest brag of all
LIKELIHOOD TO DIE Low
BEST TIME TO GO Year-round
PHYSICAL DIFFICULTY Low
COST Free

Whether you call it the Western Wall, Wailing Wall, or Kotel, it is one of Israel's holiest places and a literal bedrock of Jewish faith.

The wall itself, an exposed stretch of limestone in the center of Jerusalem's old city, is not much to look at. It is, however, the last surviving remnant of the Second Temple built by Herod around 19 B.C., atop the holy hill known as Temple Mount. The entire area was considered the center of Jewish spirituality for centuries until the temple was destroyed in A.D. 70 by the Romans.

Jewish spiritual leaders say that, even after the temple's destruction, the divine presence of God will never leave the Western Wall, nor will it ever be destroyed.

Today, Jewish pilgrims from around the world visit the wall to pray and, most visibly, to mourn the fall of the temple. People kiss the stones and slip handwritten notes to God in the wall's cracks and crevices. Though the Western Wall is considered the holiest place in Judaism, people of all faiths can (and do) leave notes in the wall when they pass through Jerusalem's old city. More than a million notes and prayers are placed in the wall each year.

The Basics

The wall stretches more than 1,600 feet, but most of it is inaccessible. The section people visit runs for 187 feet and is fronted by a large open-air plaza that accommodates thousands of worshippers. Until recently, men and women were not allowed to pray together at the wall—a major point of contention for non-Orthodox Jews. In 2016, the Israeli Supreme Court approved the creation of a mixed space where men and women can now pray together.

Access to the wall is tightly controlled for both security and religious reasons; dress respectfully, which means hats or yarmulkes for men, head-covering shawls and long skirts or pants for women.

There are no restrictions on the size or style of notes left in the wall, just be respectful and avoid ostentatious displays (just say no to glitter pens and colorful paper).

THINGS TO KNOW

- ✕ Non-Jews sometimes call it the Wailing Wall because prayers offered at the wall were deeply felt, and often vocal and tearful displays of faith. However, Jews do not use the name Wailing Wall and consider it a low-grade insult.

- ✕ The Western Wall is seriously sturdy. It's easy to believe that only God's divine presence has kept it safe for more than three thousand years, during which Jerusalem was destroyed and rebuilt no fewer than nine times.

- ✕ Want to leave God a note, but can't personally travel to Jerusalem? No problem. The custom of inserting handwritten prayers into the Western Wall is so widespread that you can hire online services to insert notes on your behalf.

TRUE OR FALSE? Jerusalem is considered the holiest city on Earth by Jews, Christians, and Muslims.

Partly true. For Jews, Jerusalem was their first capital and is home to Temple Mount, site of the holiest of holy Jewish temples. For Christians, it's the site of the Last Supper and where Jesus was crucified and buried. For Muslims, while Jerusalem is an important city (where the prophet Muhammad ascended to heaven), Mecca and Medina are considered more holy.

VISIT THE NAZCA LINES

WHAT Message delivered, meaning unclear
WHERE Nazca, Peru
BRAG FACTOR Medium
LIKELIHOOD TO DIE Low
BEST TIME TO GO Year-round
PHYSICAL DIFFICULTY Medium
COST $–$$

No doubt you've seen them featured in nature-oriented magazines and television shows: intricate designs of llamas, leopards, spiders, and the occasional human sprawling across the high desert plains of Peru. These are the world-famous Nazca Lines, covering more than 170 square miles, with some of the designs spanning more than a thousand feet from top to bottom.

Painstakingly created, stone by stone, more than two thousand years ago, for unclear reasons by an ancient civilization we don't know much about, the Nazca Lines are the quintessential riddle wrapped in a mystery inside an enigma, inspiring wild speculation about their purpose.

Were they an ancient astronomical observatory? Were they offerings to sky gods? Irrigation canals? Navigational signposts for alien civilizations?

It's likely we'll never know. The lack of answers is what drives small bands of mystics and prophets to visit the site each year. Whether viewed standing on a nearby foothill or—best of all—from the air, the Nazca Lines *feel* important and meaningful. They are an elegantly designed message from the dawn of human civilization. We just don't know what the message says.

The Basics

Nazca's geoglyphs—that's the technical term for using durable landscape features such as rocks as your art canvas—were created by removing reddish-brown pebbles to expose lighter-colored soil below. It's a low-tech process that, when applied to the Nazca's artful designs, yields amazing results: hundreds of geometric designs and more than seventy large-scale images of birds and animals etched into the dry desert plains.

Nazca was recognized as a UNESCO World Heritage Site in 1994, which jump-started efforts to preserve and protect the geoglyphs. Unfortunately, the Nazca desert is at risk from global warming and changing weather patterns; scientist fear a single heavy rain could wash out large sections of the site.

Given the Nazca's fragility, access to the geoglyphs is strictly off limits. Even scientists are required to wear special shoes when studying the site.

Nazca is roughly 200 miles south of Lima, Peru's capital. The simplest way to view Nazca's geoglyphs is by foot. Signposted trails crisscross the surrounding foothills, offering just enough elevation to properly admire many of the most famous designs. You can also organize fly-overs from Nazca ($150 and up) or from the cruise ship port in Paracas ($450 and up).

THINGS TO KNOW

- ✗ Who were the Nazca? They predate the Incas by as much as two thousand years. They were most likely farmers who settled in the foothills of the Andes mountains. Besides geoglyphs, the Nazca are noted for their sophisticated pottery and underground aqueducts. They died out in the eighth century A.D. for reasons that remain unclear.

- ✗ The Nazca Lines were forgotten for more than a thousand years until 1927, when a Peruvian archaeologist spotted them on a hike. It wasn't until the 1930s, when the first planes flew over the remote region, that the geoglyphs' vast scale and beauty were fully understood.

- ✗ Nazca's dry climate is credited with preserving the unattended designs for so many centuries. The average rainfall is less than 0.15 inches per year.

Besides weather, what is responsible for the greatest damage to Nazca's geoglyphs in recent years?

Greenpeace. The pro-environmental group placed a protest banner on the ground next to the famous hummingbird geoglyph. Unfortunately, the twenty or so activists also carved a new and semipermanent path, visible from the air, as they hiked to and from the off-limits site. Oops.

RETRACE THE HIPPIE TRAIL

WHAT Relive the ultimate rite of passage for freaks and beatniks
WHERE Istanbul to Kathmandu
BRAG FACTOR Medium
LIKELIHOOD TO DIE Medium
BEST TIME TO GO March–October
PHYSICAL DIFFICULTY Medium
COST $$$

If you have parents older than sixty, go ask them about the "hippie trail." They'll likely know *all* about it, because traveling the hippie trail was a rite of passage back in the late 1960s and '70s, as a way to prove you truly were a beatnik alternative nonconformist.

You can blame The Beatles. The "mystic east" had beckoned western travelers for centuries, but it took on new urgency in the afterglow of The Beatles' highly publicized 1968 sojourn in India. The Fab Four inspired a generation of twenty-something Brits, Americans, Canadians, Aussies, and Kiwis to hit the road and travel in the thousands.

The hippie trail had many routes (yes, there are many paths to self-discovery). The most iconic started in Istanbul and carved a rugged track through Iran (Tehran), Afghanistan (Herat, Kandahar, Kabul), Pakistan (Karachi, Peshawar, Lahore), India (New Delhi, Varanasi), and Nepal (Kathmandu) before veering off into the wilds of Southeast Asia.

The goal was always to travel as cheaply as possible, in order to travel for as long as possible. Air travel was in its infancy and prohibitively expensive, so overland journeys by bus, car, Volkswagen van, or even motorbike were the norm on the hippie trail. An entire generation discovered the love of travel, for travel's sake, along the way.

The Basics

Iran, Afghanistan, Pakistan . . . these are not countries at the top of today's travel wish lists. But don't be deterred. Yes, Afghanistan looks closed to Westerners for the foreseeable future. But Turkey, India, and Nepal are relatively easy destinations to tackle. You can retrace the entire hippie trail in these countries with absolutely no problem.

Even Iran is not out of reach. The trick is having money. Travel agencies will organize individual visas and smooth paperwork roadblocks in Iran, but it will cost you. Alternatively, book a group tour. It's as unhippie as you can get, but it's the simplest way to keep Iran on your itinerary.

THINGS TO KNOW

- × It's no coincidence the hippie trail passed through the world's major hashish-producing regions. Getting high was an accepted part of life on the hippie trail.

- × Kathmandu was famous for its legal pot shops. Hash remained legal in Nepal until 1973.

- × The hippie trail was popular in an era before Lonely Planet guidebooks and before—gasp!—Facebook and the Internet. So how did travelers share information? They did it via physical bulletin boards. Istanbul's Pudding Shop, a cafe that was once near the Blue Mosque but has long since gone, was possibly the most famous meet-up and info-sharing spot along the entire hippie trail.

- × All good things come to an end. The hippie trail's end came abruptly in 1979, following the Islamic revolution in Iran and the Soviet invasion of Afghanistan. The overland trail was closed . . . though hopefully not forever.

TRUE OR FALSE? The travel company Lonely Planet was originally called Lovely Planet.

Partly true. Founders Tony and Maureen Wheeler named their company Lonely Planet after a corrupted line in the Joe Cocker song "Space Captain." Joe Cocker sang the words lovely planet, Tony Wheeler heard "lonely planet," and the rest is history.

PERFORM THE HAJJ

WHAT Join the world's largest annual gathering of people
WHERE Mecca, Saudi Arabia
BRAG FACTOR For Muslims, there is no higher religious duty
LIKELIHOOD TO DIE Low
BEST TIME TO GO Last month in the Islamic year (varies)
PHYSICAL DIFFICULTY Medium
COST $–$$

At its annual peak—over five days in the last month of the Islamic year—Mecca hosts the planet's largest gathering of people: more than two million devout Muslims looking to God to forgive their sins and bless their once-in-a-lifetime journey.

The hajj, the act of making a pilgrimage to Mecca, is not just a good idea for Muslims, it's a religious requirement. Every adult Muslim must undertake the pilgrimage to Mecca at least once in their lifetime, assuming they have the financial and physical abilities to do so. The latter is key: The hajj can be physically and mentally demanding.

Undertaking the hajj means performing a series of religious rituals. It also means, for the duration of your stay in Mecca, wearing modest clothes, no swearing, no spitting, no smoking, no shaving, and no sex. Pilgrims start by entering ihram, a state of holiness that's signified by wearing two white cloths, one around your waist and one over your upper body, and simple sandals.

Next you walk counterclockwise, seven times, around the Ka'aba, the black cube-shaped building at the heart of Mecca. This is followed by walking back and forth seven times between the hills of Safa and Marwah, which is a shorter distance than it sounds (the entire path is enclosed in a long walkway).

Before the hajj is complete, pilgrims will perform a ritual stoning of the devil (by throwing pebbles at a series of stone pillars), shave their heads (women can have a small lock of hair removed), and offer an animal sacrifice to God (so-called sacrifice vouchers make it easy to purchase shares of a lamb or camel to be slaughtered by somebody else).

The Basics

If you're a non-Muslim interested in the hajj, forget about it.

Not only is Mecca off-limits to non-Muslims, the hajj itself cannot be performed by non-Muslims; doing so was once a crime punishable by death. That's no longer the case, but still—do not attempt the hajj if you are not a serious Muslim.

Mecca is in Saudi Arabia, which is not an easy country to visit for foreigners. American Muslims can apply for special hajj visas from the Saudi Arabian government as long as you have not made the pilgrimage in the prior five years.

THINGS TO KNOW

×   The Islamic calendar is lunar, which means the Islamic year is about eleven days shorter than the Gregorian year familiar to Christians. It also means hajj dates vary year to year in the Gregorian calendar.

- The hajj is held once a year. At other times, pilgrims visit Mecca and perform a lesser pilgrimage known as umrah. The umrah is no substitute for the hajj, however, so these pilgrims must return to Mecca in their lifetime to perform the major pilgrimage.

- Muslim women must travel in the company of a husband or close male relative. Only women over the age of forty-five can travel solo, and even then they must carry a letter of approval signed by their husband or father.

What is Saudi Arabia's largest annual source of income, after oil and gas?

The hajj. Saudi Arabia's government earns more than $9 billion each year from pilgrims arriving to perform the hajj.

LEARN TO FIREWALK

WHAT Everybody's doing it
WHERE Multiple Locations
BRAG FACTOR High ("I walked on fire!!")
LIKELIHOOD TO DIE Low
BEST TIME TO GO Year-round
PHYSICAL DIFFICULTY Low
STRESS LEVEL High ("Am I walking on fire?!")
COST $

Firewalking is an ancient practice, used for centuries as a rite of passage for young warriors and to demonstrate religious faith. Nowadays, it also a profitable and growing industry.

You are most likely to encounter firewalking on websites offering personal empowerment and spiritual enlightenment—not to mention team building, motivational seminars, and bachelor-party entertainment.

Beyond the hoopla and corporate marketing, firewalking is a powerful and often life-changing experience, especially for first-timers. There's nothing quite like putting your feet into a literal fire and taking the first step. And don't worry if you bail out at the last minute: Just being present and witnessing others firewalk can be a powerful experience, too.

The Basics

Firewalking is real, no gimmicks or tricks required. It's possible for two reasons (spoiler alert!). First, embers are not good conductors of heat. And second, assuming you walk quickly, your feet are not in contact with the burning embers for long enough to cause burns or blistering.

Just keep in mind the Golden Rule of firewalking: Walk, do not run.

Running pushes your feet deeper into the embers and, as a result, can cause burns on the top of your feet. All you need is proper oversight and some basic training. Except in rare cases, you are unlikely to be injured.

Firewalking is not a do-it-yourself path to enlightenment. You need an experienced coach. Companies worldwide offer half-day seminars that typically costs less than $150 and include lessons on self-empowerment (whether you want the lesson or not).

More expensive multiday courses inevitably include outdoor retreats, motivational speakers, dynamic meditation . . . pretty much spirituality in all its many forms.

THINGS TO KNOW

- ✕ Is there a career in firewalking? Of course! Become a certified firewalking instructor at one of a half-dozen US schools offering the service. The typical course lasts three to four days and costs north of $2,000. It looks great on a business card: Motivational Speaker, Life Coach, Firewalker.

- ✕ Has firewalking lost its thrill? Not to worry. Many of the same seminars and schools that offer firewalking also offer glasswalking, rebar bending, block chopping, and board breaking.

What did self-help guru Tony Robbins blame when thirty novice firewalkers reported being burned at a 2016 "Unleash the Power Within" seminar in Dallas, Texas?

The participants' lack of focus. (Nice move, Tony, to blame the innocent victims.)

EXERCISE THE SPIRIT

WHAT Om Shanti meets an awesome left break
WHERE Nicoya Peninsula, Costa Rica
BRAG FACTOR Medium
LIKELIHOOD TO DIE Low
BEST TIME TO GO December–April
PHYSICAL DIFFICULTY Low
COST $$–$$$

Pura vida literally means "pure life" in Spanish. In Costa Rica, pura vida is everywhere—on T-shirts, tourist trinkets, and splashed across roadside billboards. It embodies the Costa Rican philosophy of enjoying life slowly, keeping it simple, and appreciating one's natural surroundings.

Surfing and yoga embody this philosophy. Both value physical and mental strength, and a respect for nature and for one's body. People travel from around the world to Costa Rica to experience pura vida through exercising mind and body together, in soulful harmony, at surf and yoga retreats.

The Nicoya Peninsula, on Costa Rica's Pacific coast, is a blissful stretch of rugged mountains that drop steeply into the Pacific Ocean, carving hundreds of postcard-perfect beaches where mountain meets the sea.

Most roads are unpaved. Intentional or not, Nicoya's lack of infrastructure protects it from the worst excesses of mass-market tourism. Of course, there are pizza places and tourist shops along Nicoya's seventy-five-mile coastline. But for now, Nicoya is where chilled-out surfers come for consistent waves and where contemplative yoga retreats beckon with oceanfront studios and eco-friendly cabins nestled in the jungle.

The Basics

Yoga retreats and surf camps are offered at low-key resorts up and down the Nicoya Peninsula. While not every aspiring yogi is a surfer, and not every surfer does yoga, programs are often combined in multiday or multiweek packages. Expect to spend $1,200 and up for a full week (including accommodation, food, and yoga/surfing).

Long-established Nicoya Peninsula resorts include the Nosara Yoga Institute in Nosara; Blue Spirit and Harmony in Playa Guiones; Pranamar and Florblanca in Santa Teresa; and Anamaya and Ylang Ylang in Montezuma.

There are few paved roads on Nicoya's southwest coast; it's rough and slow going. You can fly into Nicoya from the international airports in San Jose and Liberia, with daily flights arriving at a tiny jungle-strip airport in Tambor.

Nicoya's dry season runs December through late April; expect plenty of sunshine and clear skies. A semiwet season runs May through August. Many tourists stay away, and locals hunker down during the serious rainy season from September through early November.

THINGS TO KNOW

- ✖ The Nicoya Peninsula is one of only four so-called Blue Zones in the world, where people live longer and are, statistically speaking, happier. Other Blue Zones include Sardinia (Italy), Okinawa (Japan), and Icaria (Greece).

- ✖ Scientists can't say exactly why Nicoyans are among the longest-living and healthiest people on Earth. That said, all Blue Zones share some characteristics: low rates of smoking, semivegetarian diets, high consumption of legumes, constant moderate physical activity, and strong family and social engagement.

TRUE OR FALSE? Costa Rica is the only country in Central America without an army.

True. Costa Rica has no army, navy, or air force. There are local police forces but no national defense force. The military was abolished by a left-leaning, farsighted president of Costa Rica in 1948.

MAKE THE SHIKOKU PILGRIMAGE

WHAT Eighty-eight stops on the path to enlightenment
WHERE Shikoku, Japan
BRAG FACTOR Medium
LIKELIHOOD TO DIE Low
BEST TIME TO GO October–November
PHYSICAL DIFFICULTY High (if you visit all eighty-eight temples in one go)
STRESS LEVEL Low
COST $$–$$$

Pilgrims come to Shikoku, the smallest of Japan's four main islands, to follow in the footsteps of Kōbō Daishi, the ninth-century monk who founded the Shingon sect of Buddhism. The complete pilgrimage consists of a circuit of eighty-eight temples, mostly around the perimeter of Shikoku. Traditional pilgrims don white robes and conical straw hats, and carry a walking stick that identifies them as a pilgrim.

The Shikoku temple circuit is one of the oldest and most famous pilgrimage routes in Japan; on foot it takes more than a month to complete. The route passes through congested cities and pristine coastal countryside, along busy urban roads and down empty mountain paths and open fields.

Each temple along the way has its own customs and rituals for pilgrims to follow, adding to the spiritual adventure. Guesthouses and campsites on the route provide easy opportunities to meet fellow travelers on their own quest for answers to life's abundant questions.

The Basics

Every year more than one hundred twenty-five thousand pilgrims tackle the Shikoku temple circuit, usually by car and bus. A small minority still set out the old-fashioned way, on foot, to go on a journey of nearly 750 miles that takes about six weeks to complete.

Fortunately, there is no requirement to visit all the temples in one go, or to visit them in a particular order. The goal is to visit each temple, regardless of how long it takes or how many stages you divide the pilgrimage into. It's also important to perform the appropriate ritual at each temple. Doing so earns you a literal stamp of approval (in exchange for a small fee) in your passport-like temple book.

October is the best month for walking in Shikoku, before the heavy rains and occasional typhoon hit. Bad weather and venomous snakes—notably the *mamushi*, "pit viper," and *yamakagashi*, "tiger keelback"—are the circuit's only true dangers for pilgrims.

THINGS TO KNOW

× Besides snakes, Shikoku is infamous for its (surprisingly large!) orange-legged centipedes, the *mukade*. They are venomous and appear out of nowhere on your arms and legs. If they bite you, seek medical help. While you're unlikely to die, the bites are painful and swell.

× Few non-Japanese complete the eighty-eight-temple circuit on foot. Those who attempt it will be received warmly by locals—especially if you're wearing the traditional robes and hat, and have even a barebones proficiency speaking Japanese.

× It's a long-standing tradition for locals to offer small gifts to pilgrims on foot. If offered, a gift must always be accepted (it's rude to do otherwise).

× The Shingon branch of Buddhism focuses on the Buddha's unspoken wisdom, not the teachings he delivered in public. As a result, it is highly esoteric. Enlightenment for Shingon Buddhists comes via the lifelong practices of meditation and yoga, plus the repetitive speaking of mystical phrases.

TRUE OR FALSE? Buddha was a real, living person.

True. Siddhartha Gautama was a fifth century B.C. monk, an enlightened teacher, and the founding figure of global Buddhism. Extra credit if you know that, according to the Buddha, desire and attachment are the cause of all worldly suffering.

HOW TO DEAL WITH A VENOMOUS SNAKE BITE

BASIC

Get medical assistance. You need professional help if bitten by a highly venomous species such as rattlesnake (USA), death adder (Australia), viper (worldwide), black mamba (Africa), or tiger (worldwide).

Take note of the snake's appearance to aid identification. Do not hunt or track down the snake, but preserve the carcass if it's already dead.

Stay calm. Panic increases your heart rate and speeds the diffusion of venom through your body.

Do not drink alcohol or caffeine. These also increase your heart rate.

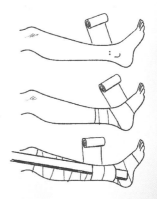

Remove any tight clothing and all jewelry. Snake bites cause rapid swelling. Constricting items may cause more issues than the bite itself.

Keep the bite area below the level of your heart. This slows blood flowing to your heart and limits the spread of venom to other parts of your body.

ADVANCED

Do not apply a tourniquet, but do everything possible to restrict movement of the bitten area. Fashion a splint with sticks, then wrap in a piece of cloth or clothing to keep the splint in place.

Do not use ice on the wound. Cold reduces the healthy circulation of blood to the bitten area.

Do not apply a suction pump to the wound. While once common practice, suction pumps are no longer considered effective (they remove no more than a third of venom from the body) and, when used improperly, can permanently damage tissue and cause infection.

Wait it out. Most snakes do not inject enough venom to be fatal to an adult human. Stay calm and wait for the venom to leave your system.

If you're in the wilderness with no chance of medical help, move as little as possible and keep your heart rate as slow as possible.

MASTER THE ART OF SILENCE

WHAT The courage to look at yourself honestly and gently
WHERE Dharamsala, India
BRAG FACTOR Medium (no bragging out loud, please)
LIKELIHOOD TO DIE Low
BEST TIME TO GO Year-round
PHYSICAL DIFFICULTY Medium
COST $

Stop for a moment and ask yourself: What's the longest you've been silent, truly silent, in the past ten years?

It's hard to be silent, even for just a few precious moments. Friends, parents, random people on the street—people talk all the time. There is no hiding from the fast-flowing torrent of words swirling around us all day and every day.

Now imagine you stop talking . . . for ten full days! No words, no conversations, no questions. Just beautiful and joyful silence for ten days.

Such is the goal of a Vipassana meditation course. Vipassana is an ancient form of Buddhist meditation. Practitioners strive to see things as they truly are, and achieve self-transformation through intense bouts of self-observation.

The Vipassana regimen is not easy. You live in a simple retreat, eating just two meals and meditating for up to ten hours per day. You utter not a single word. Most people say it is one of the most physically, emotionally, and mentally challenging experiences of their lives. Ten days later you emerge, having quieted your inner voice, grateful, mindful, positive, and kind.

The Basics

While Vipassana training is offered by innumerable teachers worldwide, the global network of Vipassana centers founded by guru Satya Narayan Goenka are the most prominent and are hugely popular. The guru passed away in 2013, but his legacy continues at more than 175 locations.

The city of Dharamsala, home in exile to the Dalai Lama, is tucked away in the forested mountains of northern India and is an excellent place to experience Vipassana. Each day includes ten hours of meditation. By the fourth day your mind is calm and focused. You learn to accept pain (from sitting cross-legged for ten hours) and to quiet voices of self-doubt in your head complaining of hunger or fatigue. By the tenth and final day, you learn to be content with your situation, whatever it may be, and depart with a deep-felt sense of goodwill toward all.

The typical course lasts twelve days: a day for orientation, ten days of silent meditation, and one day for wrapping up. There is no direct cost; all meals and accommodations are free. Vipassana centers work on a pay-it-forward model. If you're content with the experience, you're encouraged to donate toward the cost of the next student.

THINGS TO KNOW

× Why do courses always last ten days? Apparently ten days is the *minimum* amount of time it takes the modern mind to settle down and focus.

× Vipassana is a nonsectarian practice, which means it is not affiliated with any specific religion. Hindus, Christians, Jews, Muslims, Jains—people of all religions are welcome to practice.

× Do people drop out before the ten days are over? It does happen. Though you won't be ostracized for leaving early, the point of the experience is to make it through ten days of silent meditation.

TRUE OR FALSE? The actor Richard Gere is a Buddhist, and his teacher is the Dalai Lama.

True. Gere considers the Dalai Lama to be his "root guru." They are sometimes spotted together on the streets of Dharamsala.

EXPERIENCE PURE EMPTINESS

WHAT No sensory inputs, no problem!
WHERE The dark recesses of your mind
BRAG FACTOR Medium
LIKELIHOOD TO DIE Low
BEST TIME TO GO Year-round
PHYSICAL DIFFICULTY Low
COST $

For most people, sensory deprivation sounds like a CIA torture method. Why would anybody willingly deprive their senses—all their senses—of inputs? No sights, no sounds, no smells or tastes, and no sense of feeling. Deprived of sensory inputs, you basically turn into a chatterbox of consciousness floating alone in the dark.

However, it turns out that short stints in sensory-deprivation tanks and pools can be highly therapeutic.

Yes, long-term exposure does lead to anxiety and depression. But in just the right amounts (usually less than ninety minutes) it can be deeply relaxing. Your heartbeat slows, your breathing is deep and even, and your brain waves start to mimic those of a yogi in deep meditation.

You'll inevitably fight the experience for the first fifteen minutes or so. "What am I doing here? Is this working? Hello, is anybody out there?!" Then the magic happens. Your brain switches gears and you begin to relax. You may even hallucinate. Next stop: Creativity Land.

The Basics

Sensory-deprivation tanks, first developed in the late 1950s, are back in fashion at high-end spas and even at dedicated "float centers" in open-minded cities such as Portland and San Francisco.

Modern sensory-deprivation tanks are nothing like their cumbersome forerunners; today's tanks are actually sleek pods, large enough for any adult to freely float in water saturated with Epsom salts (simultaneously to make you buoyant and to prevent drownings). Insert earplugs, close the door, and immerse your naked self in total darkness. The water is kept at the average temperature of skin (about 93 degrees Fahrenheit).

The cost is usually less than $100 for a ninety-minute session.

THINGS TO KNOW

- Experiments show that your brain waves change inside a flotation tank. The alpha and beta waves of a healthy, conscious mind give way to the theta waves experienced right before falling asleep. Your visual cortex also becomes more active.

- Sensory deprivation can foster creativity and enhance performance in tasks that require high levels of concentration. In one study, jazz musicians enhanced their motor and technical skills after just sixty minutes in a float tank.

- Students who spend time in a flotation tank also do better on tests, according to studies.

In the 1980 film *Altered States*, directed by Ken Russell and starring William Hurt, what happens when a Harvard scientist starts taking hardcore hallucinogenic drugs inside his isolation tank?

Nothing good. William Hurt's character manages to access an alternate reality, transforms himself into a gorilla, then into a primordial human, then into an amorphous ball of energy, before nearly evaporating into an alternate dimension of space. Fortunately, the love of a good woman saves him.

CONNECT WITH DREAMTIME

WHAT We are all visitors to this time, this place. We are just passing through.

WHERE Uluru, Australia

BRAG FACTOR Low

LIKELIHOOD TO DIE Low

BEST TIME TO GO May–September

PHYSICAL DIFFICULTY Medium

COST $–$$$

To the Aboriginal inhabitants of Australia, Uluru is more than just a massive, red-hued outcrop of sandstone. Aboriginal Australians believe in the concept of dreamtime, when the world was featureless and when the gods and all living things intermingled. Ancient ancestors emerged from the void of dreamtime and created the landscapes and people of Earth.

Of the many sacred Aboriginal sites in Australia, few are as important as Uluru—it is living evidence of the ancestors' activities during the dreamtime creation period.

The local Yankunytjatjara and Pitjantjatjara people believe the record of dreamtime lives in the rock itself: Specific outcroppings represent the literal incarnation of ancestral spirits. Touching the rocks invokes these spirits and opens a direct line of communication and communion with dreamtime.

Beyond its spiritual side, Uluru is also visually stunning, rising more than a thousand feet above an otherwise barren desert landscape. It glows bright red at sunrise and sunset, and fades to purple when it rains (thanks to a chemical reaction with the sandstone).

It's also the main tourism draw for literally hundreds of miles in every direction. Without Uluru and the nearby rock formations at Kata Tjuta, it's a safe bet most tourists wouldn't bother with the arduous journey to central Australia.

The Basics

The history of Uluru is controversial. For many years, white Australians called it Ayers Rock and paid little attention to the cultural sensitivities of local Aboriginal people. The state government allowed people to climb Ayers Rock (a sensitive point with Aboriginals). Photographs were allowed (another sensitive point). And only minimal efforts were made to preserve artifacts and cave paintings.

On the plus side, the Australian government returned ownership of Uluru to the local Aborigines in 1985 (it's leased back to Australia's national parks through 2084). Climbing is now officially discouraged, at least on the most sensitive parts of Uluru. Photography is forbidden in many sections. And tourism agencies make efforts to engage (and often employ) local Aborigines to share their stories and dreamtime ceremonies.

The Uluru-Kata Tjuta National Park was designated a UNESCO World Heritage Site in 1987. Visitors arrive via Alice Springs, the nearest city (though "near" is a misnomer—it's more than 280 miles away) or by plane directly into Ayers Rock Airport, a twenty-minute drive to the national park.

The best time to visit is May through September when the weather is cooler and there's a chance of catching a seasonal waterfall or two.

THINGS TO KNOW

- × Uluru is like an iceberg—most of its bulk lies underground and out of view. It's what is geologically known as an inselberg, formed millions of years ago as a former mountain range was eroded slowly over eons.

- × Kata Tjuta, Uluru, and the surrounding town of Ayers Rock have plenty to offer travelers: skydives, helicopter flights, camel treks, guided hikes—even an outdoor restaurant where you can dine under the stars, in the shadow of Uluru.

- × You may meet Blue-Tongue Lizard Man if you're lucky enough to spend time with Aborigines at Uluru or observe a dreamtime ceremony. Blue-Tongue Lizard Man is a mythical sorcerer who summoned a magic fire to chase his sons, who mistakenly killed a sacred kangaroo. Today, Blue-Tongue Lizard Man's spirit is rekindled in fire ceremonies, when young Aboriginal warriors emerge from darkness into the glow of a ceremonial fire.

TRUE OR FALSE? There are more than seven hundred fifty thousand wild camels roaming Australia's Outback.

True. Camels were imported from India in the nineteenth century to transport goods across Australia's desert regions. Nowadays they're a huge ecological problem, largely because they consume vast quantities of water and have no natural predators.

WORSHIP THE SUNRISE

WHAT Stand and greet the dawn
WHERE Amesbury, England
BRAG FACTOR Low
LIKELIHOOD TO DIE Low
BEST TIME TO GO Summer and winter solstices
PHYSICAL DIFFICULTY Low
COST $–$$

The standing stones at Stonehenge are, without a doubt, the world's most famous ancient astronomical monument.

It also helps that Stonehenge is dramatically photogenic. Towering stones—some more than 14 feet tall and 6 feet wide—form a massive concentric ring and perfectly align with the rising sun on the winter and summer solstices. At these times, people gather in the hundreds (occasionally thousands) to sing, dance, pray, party, and perform the odd druid ritual or witch's spell.

Few people have the privilege of observing a solstice from inside the Stonehenge monument, with the sun rising directly above the so-called Heel Stone that lies just beyond the inner circle. Those who are lucky enough marvel at the precision of Stonehenge's ancient—and mysterious—builders. Clearly, Stonehenge is a place to observe and honor the giver of all life, the sun.

Stonehenge was built in phases between 3000 and 2000 B.C. The site encompasses much more than the famous concentric stones. It's surrounded by burial mounds and a network of roads and neolithic villages used by those who built the monument. They came from across ancient Britain, from as far away as the Scottish Highlands, based on remains found at the site.

The Basics

For many years, it was possible to walk right up to the stones, even to climb on them. The stones were roped off in the late 1970s and, today, touching is strictly prohibited. There's still plenty of room to walk among the stones and explore for a small fee.

Private tours that get you inside the roped-off sections are available (usually on a day trip from London) for less than $150 per person.

THINGS TO KNOW

- Druid temple? Alien landing site? Ancient burial ground? The true purpose of Stonehenge may never be known. Among scientists, the current leading theory is Stonehenge was the terminus of an ancient funerary route, a place to bring the dead on their final journey into the great beyond.

- It's long been thought that the so-called bluestones, which form Stonehenge's innermost ring, came from Wales, more than 140 miles to the northwest, and were transported to the current site using primitive Stone Age technology, possibly floated on rafts or rolled over wooden poles, conveyor-belt style.

- Numerous baseball-sized stones, polished by human hands, have been found buried at the site. Some archaeologists think Stonehenge was built using these primitive ball bearings, the stones transported atop a cushion of rolling stones.

- Before the megapopular Glastonbury music festival, there was the Stonehenge Free Festival. It was held each June from 1974 to 1984 on the grounds of Stonehenge. The festival ended on the summer solstice—quite a finale!

According to David St. Hubbins, lead singer for the band Spinal Tap, what was the problem with the handcrafted model of Stonehenge used during the live performance of their eponymous song, "Stonehenge"?

It was in danger of being crushed by a dwarf.

SLOW IT WAY DOWN

WHAT Mindfulness in travel
WHERE Your next vacation
BRAG FACTOR Low
LIKELIHOOD TO DIE Low
BEST TIME TO GO Year-round
PHYSICAL DIFFICULTY Low
COST Think of the benefits, not the costs

"Slow travel" is an offshoot of the slow food movement, which began in Italy in the 1980s as a protest against the opening of a McDonald's in Rome. The founder of the slow food movement, Carlo Petrini, argues that modern humans believe life is short and that we must go faster to fit in everything. But life is long. Our problem is we have forgotten how to spend our time wisely.

The easiest way to be a slow traveler? On your next trip, book a local accommodation in a nontouristy neighborhood, stick to locally owned cafés and restaurants, eat regional produce, use local transit, and visit places not found in any guidebook.

Slow travel is about independence and not feeling pressure to "see it all." It's about staying in fewer places for longer stretches, choosing local accommodations over chain hotels, having flexible travel dates, waking up with no set itinerary, skipping that popular tourist attraction and instead seeing what adventures unfold that day. Slow travelers seek out local cuisine and entertainment, and make sincere efforts to meet local people and experience their culture.

The Basics

Many people are confused about slow travel. They think it means traveling longer, choosing to be uncomfortable, forsaking all creature comforts. Nope.

Slow travel is about making conscious choices. It is about slowing down rather than speeding up. It's about connecting to a place and its people. The journey itself becomes an opportunity to experience and engage, rather than to be merely tolerated. Slow travel is a mindset that rejects traditional ideas of tourism.

To participate means choosing experiences over sights and quality over quantity. The journey is not an inconvenience. Savor the things that happen en route, and take the time to experience and enjoy wherever you are.

THINGS TO KNOW

- ✗ In 2016, an estimated 3.6 billion passengers flew on commercial jets. That's nearly 10 million people a day in the skies above Earth, not traveling slowly.

- ✗ Airplanes are the bane of slow travel. Blame Pan American World Airways. It was the launch customer and first US airline to fly Boeing's groundbreaking 707 jet airliner, which kicked off the jet age and made air travel affordable to the masses. Pan Am's inaugural flight—New York to Paris (with a refueling stop in Newfoundland)—took off on October 26, 1958 and cost $248 round-trip.

- ✗ The ideal transport for a slow traveler? Possibly the donkey. It's faster than a camel, and can carry more—and eats less—than a horse. If donkeys are good enough for Don Quixote, they're good enough for modern slow travelers.

How long does it take to walk around the world?

Roughly eleven years. At least that's how long it took a Canadian man, Jean Béliveau, to walk from Montreal and back between 2000 and 2011. He covered sixty-four countries on a circuitous route through Central and South America, Africa, Western Europe, the Middle East, across the Indian Subcontinent, China, Southeast Asia, and Australia before ending up back in North America. He wore through sixty-four pairs of shoes on his forty-seven-thousand-mile odyssey.

WORSHIP IN THE TEMPLE OF WILDERNESS

WHAT We are all travelers in the wilderness of this world
WHERE Waretown, New Jersey
BRAG FACTOR Medium
LIKELIHOOD TO DIE Low
BEST TIME TO GO Year-round
PHYSICAL DIFFICULTY Medium–High
COST $$

Cable television has done a disservice to wilderness survival. Thanks to shows such as *Survivorman*, *Out of the Wild*, and the truly awful *Fat Guys in the Woods*, the pop-culture view of wilderness survival is warped. It teaches how to muscle your way through adversity and push your body to the very edge of what it can handle. It's reality television with all brawn and no brain.

That's not how Tom Brown Jr. approaches the wilderness. His Tracker School focuses on three core survival skills: tracking, nature observation, and awareness. Brown adds equal emphasis to the spiritual side of survival based on the teachings of Stalking Wolf, an Apache elder who taught the young Brown his mad-dog survival skills.

Tracker School is not unique. Many wilderness programs teach spirituality alongside hardcore survivalism. Brown's take is interesting largely because he, himself, is so relentlessly interesting.

After his mentor Stalking Wolf died, Brown spent the next ten years living rough in the woods, fully off the grid (no manufactured tools, no prefab tent, no clothes except what nature provided). Brown was directionless after he emerged shirtless and shoeless from the woods, until a local sheriff called him to track a missing person.

Brown has since found forty missing persons, helped investigate four murders, written eighteen survival books, and produced two survival-oriented movies.

The Basics

Tracker School is based in New Jersey, with occasional courses offered in California. Most people start with a six-day class in basic survival, learning how to build a primitive shelter, find water, make a bow-drill fire, and find food. Advanced classes focus on making a home in any wilderness environment: living in a debris hut, making wood-burned bowls and spoons, fashioning clothes from plants—that sort of thing.

Other courses focus on healing, scouting, and tracking both animals and people. And, of course for the ultimate in wilderness spirituality, there are courses on prophecy, shamanic vision quests, traveling into the past, probing the future, preparing for the Exodus, prepping for the end of days, and how to locate worldwide safe places and escape from Armageddon.

Classes cost $800 and up and include food and rough living in the great outdoors.

THINGS TO KNOW

× Tom Brown Jr. is best known for his tracking skills using footprints and clues left behind on any surface in nature. It's said he can tell a person's size, sex, weight, hair color, whether they're right- or left-handed, and their emotional state.

× Urban warriors are welcome at Tracker School. Consider a course in psychological warfare, wolverine fighting, and suburban survival.

× Brown and his Tracker School are not without controversy. One infamous case involved a $5 million lawsuit against Brown for tracking and identifying the wrong person in a rape case. The incident got Brown a hot-seat interview on the *Today Show*.

How long can you survive without air, food, or water?

For air the record is eleven minutes, for water it's eighteen days, for food it's seventy-four days.

HOW TO START A FIRE IN DIFFICULT CONDITIONS

BASIC

Build a fire. A standard fire has five ingredients. First is a fire bed, dug a few inches below ground (windy conditions) or on a small mound of dirt (nonwindy). Second is tinder, easily combustible material such as dry leaves, bark, grass, or fungi. Third is kindling, dry twigs or small branches that burn easily and longer than tinder. Fourth is fuel wood, dry large logs or branches to keep the fire going. Fifth is a fire-starter such as matches.

In wet conditions, use a knife to remove the top layers of bark from kindling and fuel wood. Use petroleum jelly, kerosene, or hand sanitizer as a fire accelerant on wet tinder.

Use a hand drill to start a fire without matches. Carve a V-shaped notch into the edge of a dry, flat piece of wood. Use a tall, thin, sturdy stick as a spindle; rotate it quickly in your hands, pressing hard into the wood immediately next to the

notch. Friction eventually produces red-hot embers that you gently blow or transfer onto tinder.

Alternatively, use a magnifying glass, eyeglasses, or binoculars as a lens to concentrate sunlight onto your tinder. Or use a plastic water bottle by holding it upside down, slowly moving it away from your tinder and adjusting the bottle's angle to magnify the sunlight.

ADVANCED

Rub toothpaste or chocolate onto the bottom of a soda can. Polish with a cloth or piece of fungus until it shines. Point the bottom of the can at the sun and place your tinder at the focal point of the reflected light.

In icy conditions, freeze clean water into a 2-inch-thick block of ice. Use a knife to whittle it into a rough lens shape, thicker in the middle and thinner on the edges. As long as the ice is clear (no dirt or impurities), it will work just like a lens to focus sunlight.

Use a condom in emergencies. Fill it with water and tie off the end. Make it as spherical as possible, adjusting the shape to create the sharpest-possible circle of concentrated sunlight. It works like a magnifying glass.

MOVE FAR FROM
THE MADDING CROWD

WHAT If you're lonely when you're alone, you're in bad company

WHERE Tristan da Cunha

BRAG FACTOR High

LIKELIHOOD TO DIE Low (not counting boredom)

BEST TIME TO GO November–March

PHYSICAL DIFFICULTY Medium

COST $$$$

Many places take pride in being remote. Yet few places can honestly claim they are the most remote.

The honor belongs to Tristan da Cunha, a speck of land in the middle of the Atlantic Ocean. It's more than 1,200 miles from the nearest inhabited land (the island of St. Helena) and more than 1,500 miles from mainland Africa. There is no air service to Tristan. By ship it takes at least seven days, in often-treacherous water, from the closest major port at Cape Town, South Africa.

When they say "remote," they are not kidding.

The island's most recent census counted 260 people plus a smattering of cattle, sheep, and pigs. The rocky soil is unproductive; potatoes (Tristan's staple food) are the only crop that reliably grows. Unfortunately, there are too few farmers on the island to guarantee self-sufficiency. The island's government posted a job listing for an Agricultural Advisor in British newspapers in 2016, hoping to entice an experienced farmer on a two-year assignment. No qualified applicants applied.

On the upside, the scenery is excellent, there is plenty of time for long walks around the island's volcanic core, wildlife (yellow-nosed albatross and rockhopper penguins) is abundant, the friendly locals speak English, and the main village boasts a pub, café, dance hall, swimming pool, and museum. Plus, there is always an abundant supply of potatoes for sale at the island's lone grocer's shop.

Tristan isn't for everybody. But it's just the thing if you crave time away . . . far from crowds and the noisome trappings of modern life. If you can reliably grow potatoes, you may never want to leave.

The Basics

Tristan da Cunha is the name of both the archipelago and its main island. Since 1816 it's been a possession of the United Kingdom. It was annexed by the British specifically to prevent the French from using Tristan as a base to rescue Napoleon Bonaparte from prison on St. Helena.

The British influence means locals speak English, use the British pound for currency, and drive on the left side of the road.

Trips to Earth's most isolated community must be well planned. Because of poor weather and rough seas, Tristan's harbor is accessible for just sixty days a year. Many would-be visitors have sailed to Tristan, but failed to land. Most tourists book passage on the half-dozen cruise ships that visit each year.

THINGS TO KNOW

- ✕ Not a single ship visited Tristan da Cunha for ten years between 1909 and 1919. The island's absolute isolation was broken only when a British steamer stopped to inform locals of the outcome of World War I (we won!).

- ✕ Tristan da Cunha has Internet service but, until recently, online retailers would not deliver packages. Remote location was not the issue. The problem was the lack of a post code. Britain's post office remedied the situation in 2005 and issued the island a post code, TDCU 1ZZ.

TRUE OR FALSE? Tristan da Cunha's first permanent settler, in 1810, was from Salem, Massachusetts.

True. Americans used the island as a naval base against the British during the War of 1812. That first American settler went on to claim Tristan for himself and optimistically renamed the archipelago the Islands of Refreshment.

GET HIGH WITH A SHAMAN

WHAT Vomit, cry, and become one with the universe
WHERE Multiple locations
BRAG FACTOR Medium
LIKELIHOOD TO DIE Low (not zero)
BEST TIME TO GO Year-round
PHYSICAL DIFFICULTY High
COST $–$$$

Ayahuasca is all the rage in Hollywood and Silicon Valley. According to its boosters, the ancient hallucinogenic brew from South America has numerous medical benefits: fighting alcoholism, managing symptoms of autism and depression, even suppressing migraine headaches.

Ayahuasca's spiritual benefits are also legendary: compassion, connectedness, openness to the divine in every living soul. People who have ingested ayahuasca happily rave about the true nature of the universe. They often experience a spiritual awakening, a deep sense of belonging, and access to higher dimensions and the occasional encounter with extradimensional astral beings.

The downside? After forty-five minutes or so, once the ayahuasca takes effect, you'll probably vomit uncontrollably. You may cry. You may have urgent diarrhea. Your heart will beat faster. You may feel as if your body is being painfully torn limb from limb . . . and then, hello sense of peaceful oneness!

For many people, drinking ayahuasca is a life-changing experience. Each hallucinogenic trip is like a decade of therapy condensed into six hours. Ayahuasca unlocks the gateway to self-healing.

In the 1960s, people would drop acid and take psychedelic "trips"; people who take ayahuasca do so in ceremonies led by shamans and faith healers. Having an experienced guide is important, especially for newcomers to ayahuasca, given all the vomiting the drug can provoke.

The Basics

Ayahuasca is a hallucinogenic tea made from boiling *Banisteriopsis caapi* vines and with leaves from the chacruna bush. It's the resulting slurry of *dimethyltryptamine* (DMT) that delivers the brew's hallucinogenic punch. Ayahuasca experiences typically last six to eight hours, depending on the tea's potency.

The constituent ingredients of ayahuasca (*Banisteriopsis caapi* vines and chacruna leaves) are perfectly legal. However, DMT and its derivatives are a Schedule I drug in the United States, which means ayahuasca is illegal and considered as dangerous as heroin.

There is no scientific data about overdoses or the long-term effects of ayahuasca. That said, a handful of deaths—mainly on the backpacker circuit in South America—have been reported in the international media. It's a sobering reminder that taking hallucinogenic drugs is dangerous and potentially lethal.

Ayahuasca retreats are now trendy in Peru, Ecuador, and Brazil; they're also popping up in the United States and Europe, though on less firm legal grounds. The typical retreat is a multiday, all-encompassing experience; two or three ayahuasca ceremonies spread over six or seven days, intermixed with meditation and a multitude of exercises in self-healing. Multiday retreats cost about $1,000 and up.

Be warned that not all ayahuasca retreats are created equal. In Peru, for example, about twenty are licensed with local authorities to host foreigners, but at least a hundred are currently operating illegally.

THINGS TO KNOW

- ✗ Ayahuasca's main psychoactive ingredient, DMT, is produced in chacruna leaves. But there is no high resulting from ingesting the leaves alone, because DMT rapidly degrades in the human body. It takes an enzyme from the *Banisteriopsis caapi* vine to temporarily inhibit DMT processing, giving the hallucinogen enough time to affect your brain and nervous system.

- ✗ Some respected physicians in the United States are petitioning the Food and Drug Administration to allow clinical trials of ayahuasca. Some believe it could be used in treatments for cancer and Parkinson's disease.

- ✗ Is there an upside to uncontrollable vomiting? Yes! The intense vomiting and diarrhea associated with ayahuasca can clear worms and harmful parasites from your intestines.

- ✗ Thanks to celebrity endorsements from the likes of Sting, Susan Sarandon, and Lindsay Lohan, ayahuasca is hugely trendy. There are ayahuasca meetups and support groups in dozens of cities across the United States.

What 2012 film, starring Jennifer Aniston, brought ayahuasca into mainstream culture?

Wanderlust. The drug was also prominently featured in the television series Weeds and Nip/Tuck.

Adventure Skill

HOW TO SURVIVE A DRUG OVERDOSE

BASIC

Call an ambulance or urgently seek medical help if there's any risk of overdose. The most important thing is to act immediately.

If the person is conscious, walk them around, keep them awake, and monitor their breathing. You can put them under a cool shower to wake them, but keep water away from their nose and mouth.

If the person is unconscious, try to wake them up. Never let them "sleep it off" as it takes only a few minutes to stop breathing and die.

Never leave an unconscious person on their back. Minimize the risk of choking if they vomit by turning them to one side.

Never put an unconscious person into a bath. Cold water could send them into shock, or they could drown.

Do not mix drugs. Antidepressants and even over-the-counter cold medicines with ephedrine or caffeine can cause unexpected reactions when mixed with illegal recreational drugs.

Start with conservative doses if you're a first-time user, when you are sick, or have taken a break from using.

Use less if you are unsure of a drug's purity. Illicit drugs are often blended with cheaper drugs or nondrug substances that can be dangerous.

ADVANCED

Heroin, opiates, and so-called downers affect the body's central nervous system. Signs of a possible overdose on downers include slurred speech, contracted pupils, slow breathing, low heart rate, and low body temperature. Ultimately a lack of oxygen to the brain leads to unconsciousness, coma, or death.

Speed, cocaine, ecstasy, and other stimulants increase heart rate, blood pressure, body temperature, and breathing. In overdose situations, this can lead to seizure, stroke, or heart attack.

Hallucinogens such as LSD, psilocybin mushrooms, and ayahuasca can result in severe panic attacks and depression. Overdoses are not usually life-threatening, except when the person has an underlying heart condition or high blood pressure.

WALK THE WAY OF ST. JAMES

WHAT There are no tourists on the Camino, just pilgrims who haven't yet found their way

WHERE Santiago de Compostela, Spain

BRAG FACTOR Medium

LIKELIHOOD TO DIE Low

BEST TIME TO GO June–September

PHYSICAL DIFFICULTY Medium

COST $$–$$$

The Camino de Santiago—known in English as the Way of St. James—is a network of ancient pilgrimage routes stretching across Spain, France, and Portugal, and all converging in northwest Spain at the cathedral in the town of Santiago de Compostela.

The earliest records of the pilgrimage date from the ninth century; back then, devout Christians would simply head out their front door and walk to Santiago de Compostela. The journey could take days, weeks, even months.

Today, hundreds of thousands of pilgrims make the journey each year. Most travel by foot, some by bike, and the occasional few by horse or donkey. There is no set route. Like medieval pilgrims, the idea is to set out from your house or inn, and to wend your way along the well-trod pilgrim roads to Santiago de Compostela.

It's a slow and contemplative journey. The scenery is beautiful: Many of the paths cut through mountaintop villages and across rolling fields and farmland.

The pilgrimage is, by nature, a religious event. The bulk of pilgrims set out for spiritual reasons and attend mass in churches and cathedrals along the way. However, you don't need to be Christian—or even religious—to follow the Camino de Santiago. For many, an extended break from the pressures of work and daily life is reason enough to make the pilgrimage.

The Basics

It's not difficult walking the major pilgrim routes to Santiago de Compostela. With only a few exceptions, most stages are reasonably flat on well-maintained paths.

The most popular route (expect major crowds in July and August) is the 500-mile Camino Francés, or French Way, which starts in France near Biarritz. The route has plenty of facilities for pilgrims and is well-marked. Walkers should plan for thirty-two to thirty-five walking days, and cyclists should give themselves twelve to fourteen riding days.

The Camino Portugues (Portuguese Way) is the second-most popular route. It starts in Lisbon or, more commonly, in the city of Porto. The stretch from Porto to Santiago de Compostela is 150 miles and has plenty of hostels and restaurants en route.

The Camino Primitivo (Primitive or Original Way) is the most physically challenging, as well as the most stunning route. It stretches 200 miles from Oviedo to Santiago de Compostela. The trail passes through undeveloped countryside, and up and over mountain passes, before joining up with the Camino Francés. Plan on thirteen to fifteen walking days from Oviedo.

Most pilgrims carry a *credencial*. Think of it like a souvenir passport; by the end of your journey, it will be full of stamps from the towns and hostels at which you stopped. The credencial also gets you discounted (sometimes free) pilgrims' accommodation and serves as proof that your journey followed an official route. This is important if you want to earn the *compostela*, a certificate given to those who complete at least 62 miles by foot, or 125 miles by bike, following one of the sanctioned pilgrim routes.

THINGS TO KNOW

- ✗ The largest safety risk to hikers along the Camino de Santiago? No, it's not bandits. It's blisters. Walking for thirty or more days, day after day, leads to sore feet and nasty blisters. Wear flip flops after a long day of trekking—it will air out your feet. Also include rest days in your itinerary.

- ✗ A network of hotels and hostels provide basic accommodation along the main Camino de Santiago routes, typically for less than $20 per person. In Santiago de Compostela itself, the route's final accommodation is the Hostal de los Reyes Católicos, directly opposite the city cathedral. Today, it's a luxury hotel with only a few beds reserved for pilgrims. Book early!

- ✗ Midsummer crowds are an issue, especially on the Camino Francés. Crowds are especially bad in so-called holy years when July 25, the day celebrating St. James's martyrdom, falls on a Sunday. The next holy year is in 2021.

What is St. James best known for?

Take your pick: one of the original Twelve Apostles, the first apostle to be martyred, brother of John the apostle, and the patron saint of Spain.

EMBRACE THE LIGHT

WHAT A thousand pinpricks of light in the sky
WHERE Chiang Mai, Thailand
BRAG FACTOR Medium
LIKELIHOOD TO DIE Low
BEST TIME TO GO November
PHYSICAL DIFFICULTY Low
COST $

Few experiences are as powerful as filling the darkness—both literal and figurative—with light. The promise of a new beginning from spiritual cleansing. Letting go of negativity. Reflecting on right action and mindfulness. These are the Buddhist inspirations behind the Loy Krathong festival.

The name *krathong* roughly translates as "floating basket," named after the small floating shrines made from banana leaves or spider lily plants and decorated with incense, flowers, and candles. These symbols of spiritual renewal pay respect to Buddha, and are released by the millions onto rivers and canals across Thailand and Laos. It happens each year on the night of the full moon in the twelfth month of the Thai lunar calendar (usually November in the Gregorian calendar).

In Chiang Mai, in northern Thailand, Loy Krathong is celebrated with a twist: Not just with floating lanterns, but also with *flying* lanterns during what's known as Yi Peng.

On the night of the full moon, sky lanterns known as *khom loi* are released simultaneously by the thousands. They glow like vast armies of jellyfish gently floating up and up to the moon. People cry. Buddhist monks chant and pray. Little kids smile and laugh, filled with wonder. For fifteen to twenty minutes, the darkness of a November evening is pierced by an explosion of light that moves heart and soul. It is pure magic.

The Basics

Loy Krathong is celebrated throughout Thailand and generally takes place over one or two days. In Chiang Mai, Loy Krathong and the Yi Peng sky lantern festival are celebrated together over three to four days.

To keep the crowd as local as possible, the exact date of the Yi Peng lantern release is not typically announced until one month before the event.

The largest Yi Peng celebration happens just outside of Chiang Mai at Maejo University (arrive early—it gets packed). Other Yi Peng events are held throughout Chiang Mai's old town, where nearly every building is decked out with flowers, candles, and lanterns.

THINGS TO KNOW

- If you're in Thailand during Loy Krathong, release your own krathong down a river. The banana-leaf vessels (sometimes made of bread) are sold everywhere. Just don't buy the plastic ones. Decorate yours with flowers, incense, and a coin for good luck.

- If you release a sky lantern, remember that what goes up must come down. Once the candles or fuel cells burn out, after about fifteen minutes, the lanterns float back to earth. It's a massive clean-up job. Do your part by only purchasing sky lanterns made of biodegradable rice paper.

- Don't forget to make a wish when you release your water or sky lantern.

TRUE OR FALSE? Officials in Thailand's capital, Bangkok, typically remove more than one million krathong from the city's waterways as part of Loy Krathong clean-up efforts.

GET BAPTIZED IN INDIA

WHAT Join the millions washing away sin
WHERE Haridwar, India
BRAG FACTOR Medium
LIKELIHOOD TO DIE Low
BEST TIME TO GO Dates vary
PHYSICAL DIFFICULTY Medium
COST $–$$

The Ganges River, flowing more than 1,500 miles across India and Bangladesh, is sacred to Hindus. Bathing in the river during the duodecennial (every twelfth year) Kumbh Mela festival is Auspicious with a capital *A*.

Hindus believe that sins accumulated in your past lives and current life require you to continue the cycle of life and death forever, until you are cleansed. Bathing in the Ganges during Kumbh Mela can break the cycle of rebirth and wash away *all* of your sins.

Kumbh Mela happens in four locations in India, each on a twelve-year cycle. It's said to be the largest single gathering of people on Earth; the last Kumbh Mela, held in 2016 in the city of Ujjain, attracted more than seventy-five million pilgrims over the festival's fifty-five day run.

The next Kumbh Mela, slated for the city of Haridwar in 2021, is likely to draw more than 110 million people.

The Basics

Kumbh Mela festivals happen in four locations, on staggered twelve-year cycles, which means there's a Kumbh Mela roughly every three to six years. The next full Kumbh Mela in the Ganges River happens at Haridwar in late 2021. Full Kumbh Melas take place at the confluence of the Ganges and Yamuna rivers at Allahabad in 2025; in the Godavari River at Nashik in 2027; and on the Shipra River at Ujjain in 2028.

The festivals each last for fifty-five days, usually with one or two days marked as especially auspicious for bathing.

It's India, so Kumbh Melas are chaotic and overwhelming in the best sense; millions of people sleeping in tents, holy men and *sadhus* on parade, celebrations and religious events held all day every day, whole armies of sanitation workers and police keeping people safe, thousands of volunteers managing the teeming crowd of bathers in the river. Plus, there's free food offered to everyone!

No invitation is required to partake in a Kumbh Mela river baptism. Simply show up.

THINGS TO KNOW

×   According to Hindu mythology, Kumbh Mela celebrates the victory of gods over demons in a battle for a pitcher filled with the nectar of immortality. Having captured the pitcher, the gods spilled four drops of nectar that landed in Haridwar, Allahabad, Nasik, and Ujjain.

×   Can't wait another twelve years to wash away your sins? No worries. A smaller Ardh Kumbh (Half Kumbh) Mela occurs in between the full Kumbh Melas at Haridwar and Allahabad.

×   There's also the highly auspicious Maha Kumbh Mela, which occurs in each of the four cities every 144 years.

× Yes, the Ganges River is dirty in many parts. Hindus say the river has cleansed their sins for so long, it's bound to be a little murky. To see pristine stretches of the Ganges, travel up in the Himalayas to the river's source.

TRUE OR FALSE? Hindus believe in many different gods.

False. Hindus believe in one God, who happens to take on many different forms.

Adventure Skill
HOW TO SURVIVE A HUMAN STAMPEDE

BASIC

Stay on the perimeter. Avoid the dense center of a crowd.

Do not fight against the movement of a crowd. Instead, use the movement, or surge, to move diagonally between pockets of people. A few steps sideways, another surge, etc., until you reach the periphery.

Put obstacles or buildings between you and the crowd's core. Move to elevated ground if possible.

Avoid walls, barricades, and dead-end streets or alleys.

Keep your arms up and close to your chest. This creates a small space for your body and protects your chest and lungs.

If you fall, get up quickly.

If you are with kids, lift them up or place them on your shoulders.

ADVANCED

Do not blindly follow others. People make poor decisions in stampede situations, clogging some exits while ignoring others.

If the crush becomes overwhelming, assume a fighter or boxer stance: arms up and out, feet spread, knees gently bent. Use a shuffle step to move and maintain balance.

If you cannot move, orient your body perpendicular to the crowd surge. Suffocation is possible when intense pressure is applied in a front-to-back direction on your chest. Turn sideways and use the natural strength of your rib cage to minimize the risk.

If you fall and cannot get up, immediately assume a "crash position": kneeling, with arms protecting head and neck. Do not lay flat.

KORA AT MOUNT KAILASH

WHAT Walk in circles around Tibet's holiest peaks
WHERE Mount Kailash, Tibet
BRAG FACTOR High
LIKELIHOOD TO DIE Low (with proper preparation)
BEST TIME TO GO May–October
PHYSICAL DIFFICULTY High
COST $–$$$

Mount Kailash is among the most famous peaks in Tibet. Not only does it stand at the source of major rivers such as the Indus, Sutlej, and Karnali, Mount Kailash is also one of those rare holy places worshipped across multiple religions. Buddhists, Hindus, and Jains all consider Mount Kailash a sacred site.

Each year, thousands of pilgrims, mostly Tibetan, perform a *kora*, "circumambulation of a holy site," at Mount Kailash. It's no leisurely stroll in the park. Mount Kailash is in a remote and famously inhospitable corner of the Tibetan plateau. Just accessing the kora's starting point in the village of Darchen takes days traveling by bus or car on battered dirt roads.

Many pilgrims perform a single kora, a 32-mile circuit, in one long day, usually fifteen hours or more. Some make multiple koras over a few days, often in threes or thirteens, which are propitious numbers for Tibetans; it's said that completing 108 circuits removes the sins of one's many lifetimes and brings salvation from the endless cycle of reincarnation. Some pilgrims even perform grueling full-body prostrations (stand, kneel, prostrate, repeat), which can take nearly a month or more to complete a single circuit.

Be prepared for the intensity of the experience. The trekking is demanding and, even for tourists, emotional. For Tibetans, pilgrimage is a journey from ignorance and self-centeredness to enlightenment and a deep sense of the interconnectedness of all life. For the few hundred non-Tibetans who make the Mount Kailash kora each year, it's often regarded as a true life-changing experience.

The Basics

Most people begin the circuit around Mount Kailash from the small village of Darchen, nestled at the southern foot of Mount Kailash at an elevation of more than 15,000 feet. There's not much here beyond simple guesthouses and basic village shops. From Lhasa or Kathmandu, Darchen is a three- or four-day overland journey with few amenities en route; bring your own food, water, and camping gear.

From Darchen, it's usually a three-day trek around Mount Kailash. Day two is the hardest, as you must cross the Drolma La pass (18,500 feet); until late April this pass can be blocked by snow. Even in summer, the weather at Mount Kailash is cold and subject to extremes (clear and sunny, torrential rain, freak snowstorms).

Guided treks are the easiest way for tourists to experience the Mount Kailash kora. Standard itineraries cover two weeks ($1,800 and up) or three weeks ($2,200 and up) and depart from Lhasa.

THINGS TO KNOW

- ✕ The summit of Mount Kailash is 22,027 feet, but it has never been climbed. All religions that consider Mount Kailash a sacred site also consider it sacrilege to set foot on its summit.
- ✕ On the kora, it's easy to pick out Buddhists and Hindus from the Jains; the former walk in a clockwise direction, while Jains walk counterclockwise.
- ✕ Bön, a Buddhist-offshoot religion native to Tibet, also considers Mount Kailash sacred. Like Jains, Bön pilgrims walk counterclockwise.

✕ The Chinese government has been "improving" Tibet, officially known as the Tibet Autonomous Region, for many years, building infrastructure and encouraging large-scale migration of ethnic Chinese to Lhasa. There are rumors that China's government is working on tourism development plans for the Mount Kailash area that will, inevitably, change the experience. Visit while you can.

TRUE OR FALSE? The current Dalai Lama, Tibet's religious head and leader in exile, believes equally in meditation, Buddhist spiritualism, and science.

True. The Dalai Lama supports research into how meditation affects the brain. He also believes if science proves a Buddhist belief wrong, Buddhism must change. It's the rare religion in search of scientific truth.

EXPOSE YOUR TRUE SELF

WHAT Be in complete harmony with nature
WHERE Cap d'Agde, France
BRAG FACTOR Could go either way
LIKELIHOOD TO DIE Low
BEST TIME TO GO Year-round
PHYSICAL DIFFICULTY Low
COST $–$$

OK, first things first: Cap d'Agde is the world's largest naturist resort. And by naturist, we mean naked naked naked. Fully naked. As in, more than forty thousand people hanging out in cafés, at the grocery store, waiting in line at a shop, dining at restaurants, riding bikes, or just chillin' on the beach—all fully unclothed, completely naked, baring it all.

That's an awful lot of people doing normal things without clothes.

It definitely takes getting used to. And that's the whole point of Cap d'Agde: getting used to yourself. Naturists believe that clothes are a sort of armor and a physical barrier people place between the world and their true selves—awkward curves, jiggly bits, and all. Naturism is the freedom to be comfortable with your own body. Freedom of the body and liberation from social norms. Everyone at Cap d'Agde is naked and equal.

Of course, the experience is not for everyone. Naturism requires a high degree of tolerance. It also requires courage: Everybody here has a story about the first time they disrobed and walked naked down the street. It's universally awkward and simply part of the process of finding your true self.

And who knows, maybe your true self is OK with naked yoga on the beach or shopping for groceries in the nude. Stranger things have happened, right?

The Basics

The Village Naturiste (Naturist Village) at Cap d'Agde, on France's Mediterranean coast, is a self-contained, fenced-off complex of hotels, shops, and nightclubs with a mile-long stretch of sandy beach facing the sea. Village admission is less than $10 and you are welcome to stay for a day, a week, or a lifetime. Accommodations include a campsite, apartments, and three hotels. The rule is "naked at all times" within the village.

Oddly enough, the village is a family-friendly destination excluding a few nightclubs that don't allow children. People of all ages mix in town, on the beach, in the shops. It's a small beach town where everybody happens to be naked.

Cap d'Agde is easy to reach by train from all major cities in France. The closest international airport is across the Spanish border in Barcelona.

THINGS TO KNOW

- ✕ Each year, more than three million naked people visit and stay at Cap d'Agde.

- ✕ Don't wear a Speedo to the beach. Don't sneak clothes. You'll be asked to take them off. As the rules clearly state, "practice total nudity in the company of the other naturists."

- ✕ While public acts of sexual indecency are a no-no (and can be fined up to $15,000), there are at least six sex clubs at Cap d'Agde. In the past decade, it's gained a reputation as a swinger's paradise.

- ✕ Piercings, studs, leather, and other body accoutrements are *not* considered clothing, in case you were wondering.

Is nudity a constitutionally protected right in the United States?

No. The infamous 1991 Supreme Court case, Barnes v. Glen Theatre, Inc., ruled that nudity itself is not inherently expressive conduct (which is protected under the First Amendment). Put more simply: Nudity is a choice, not a right.

COMMUNE WITH THE NAVAJO

WHAT Journey into the Navajo's sacred tribal lands
WHERE Canyon de Chelly, Arizona
BRAG FACTOR Low
LIKELIHOOD TO DIE Low
BEST TIME TO GO September–October
PHYSICAL DIFFICULTY Low
COST $

A famous Navajo proverb says, "Be still, and the earth will speak to you." There is no place where this rings as true as the majestic Canyon de Chelly. The earth here has many stories to tell.

Canyon de Chelly is one of the few continuously inhabited landscapes of North America; its caves and canyons have been home to humans for more than five thousand years. It preserves the cliffside ruins and stone paintings of the ancient Puebloan people known as the Anasazi. And it is the historical home of the Navajo, until the tribe was brutally attacked and forced to relocate in 1863.

Today the canyon remains a Navajo sacred site, lying inside the boundaries of the modern Navajo Nation.

Canyon de Chelly is also a popular national monument, drawing crowds year-round to marvel at the dramatic vistas and viewpoints: the 800-foot-tall sandstone tower known as Spider Rock and gorges and ravines branching off in all directions. One of the park's most major and photogenic attractions is the rugged beauty of the cliffside ruins known as the White House.

Roughly two hundred Navajo still live in Canyon de Chelly. From the canyon's rims you can spot a traditional Navajo dwelling, a cone-shaped structure called a hogan, along with the often-photographed White House. Navajo medicine men still visit the White House to make offerings and pray to spirits because Canyon de Chelly is a living monument, a place where the old ways of the Navajo continue.

Over a campfire, on a canyon hike, by horseback or on foot, you can't help but soak up the canyon's history and spirituality.

The Basics

The Canyon de Chelly National Monument spans 131 square miles and includes three major canyon systems (Canyon de Chelly, Canyon del Muerto, and Monument Canyon). It's the only national monument not owned by the federal government, since it is fully inside the semi-autonomous Navajo Nation.

Only the canyon's rims and the trail to the White House ruins are accessible without a Navajo guide. Otherwise, to explore the canyon floor and the many ravines and ruins hidden within, you need a backcountry permit and must hire a Navajo guide. Navajo-operated 4x4 tours of the canyon are also available.

The national monument entrance is a few miles outside the small town of Chinle, Arizona. The park is open year-round, with late summer and early autumn offering the best chances for a not too hot, not too cold experience.

THINGS TO KNOW

- × According to Navajo legend, towering Spider Rock is home to Spider Woman, the weaver of the universe and the god who taught the Navajo the "Beauty Way" of maintaining balance in mind, body, and soul. She also takes bad children and weaves them into oblivion—so watch out!

- × Canyon de Chelly preserves the architecture and artifacts of at least four great civilizations: the Archaic people, the Basketmakers, the Anasazi (predecessors of the modern Pueblo and Hopi peoples), and the Navajo.

- × While you may not have visited Canyon de Chelly, it's very likely you've seen photos. Ansel Adams, Timothy O'Sullivan, and Edward S. Curtis all spent time here in the late nineteenth and early twentieth centuries, capturing famous images of its red sandstone towers and ruined cliffside dwellings, and of the Navajo.

TRUE OR FALSE? The Navajo language is so difficult to learn that it was used as a secret code during World War II.

True. Bilingual Navajos, known as Navajo code talkers, served mostly with the United States Marine Corps in the war's Pacific theater. Code talkers sent secret messages in Navajo, a nonwritten tonal language, which the Japanese military were not able to decode.

BOOK YOUR SPACE FUNERAL

WHAT Because every adventure must come to an end
WHERE The vacuum of space
BRAG FACTOR High
LIKELIHOOD TO DIE Death is a prerequisite
BEST TIME TO GO There's never a good time to go
PHYSICAL DIFFICULTY Low (you're dead—see above)
COST $$$- $$$$$

Yes, space burial is a thing. The pitch is simple. Do you fantasize about breaking the bonds of Earth? Do you dream of landing on the moon? Do you want to help spread humanity's presence among the stars?

A handful of private companies, mostly in the United States, offer prepackaged memorial spaceflights. You can book yourself, or the ashes of a loved one, on a dizzying variety of flights: suborbital, to the moon, even on a trajectory out of the solar system. "Remember a loved one throughout the night sky" is a marketing slogan for one service that blasts your ashes into orbit, which later burn up (intentionally) in Earth's atmosphere as a symbolic shooting star.

It's easy to roll your eyes at space burial. However, for many people—including a roster of astronauts, and scientists—there's something poetic, about casting one's ashes into the void of space.

The Basics

The first commercial space burial took off on a Pegasus rocket in 1997 and deposited the remains of twenty-four people, including *Star Trek* creator Gene Roddenberry and the 1960s counterculture hero Timothy Leary, into Earth orbit. The remains fell back to Earth and burned up in 2002.

The first lunar service, in which a rocket intentionally crashes into the Moon, followed in 1998 with the remains of planetary scientist Eugene Shoemaker. Since then, half a dozen space burials have taken flight. And many more are planned.

The service costs between $2,000 and $15,000, depending on your final destination (beyond the solar system is, understandably, the most expensive option).

After signing up, you receive a space-memorial kit via mail that includes a small space-friendly capsule. Use the miniscoop included in your kit to transfer a symbolic portion of the remains into the capsule, drop it in the mail (free shipping included!) and a company such as Celestis or Elysium Space takes care of the rest. Blast off!

THINGS TO KNOW

×   Technically, you don't need to be dead in order to have a space funeral. Companies now offer to swab your mouth and send your DNA into space. Upside: Your complete genome arrives on a distant habitable planet and you're brought back to life. Downside: Same scenario as above, but the planet is inhabited by evil aliens who enslave your clone.

×   In 2014, the first space-burial flight specifically for pets was launched. Dogs, cats, snakes—the type of pet does not matter.

×   All space burials launching in the United States are reviewed and approved by the Federal Aviation Administration. Missions must be designed so that no orbital debris ends up in space or falls back to Earth.

TRUE OR FALSE? To escape Earth's gravity, spaceships leaving the planet must travel at a minimum of 25,000 miles per hour.

True. That's known as Earth's escape velocity. The average flight into orbit takes about 8½ minutes.

Adventure Kick-Start Guides

Use the following guides as inspiration for your next vacation or weekend getaway. Close your eyes, run your finger down the list and, presto! Wherever your finger lands, go there or do that.

Visit a World-Class Museum

Smithsonian Institution Nineteen museums and galleries in Washington, DC. Highlights include the Apollo 11 command module and the Wright brothers' 1903 *Spirit of St. Louis* plane.

Uffizi Gallery Easily the world's finest collection of Renaissance art and sculpture, in the heart of Florence.

Louvre Museum It holds far more than just Leonardo da Vinci's *Mona Lisa*. The finest works from antiquity through the early nineteenth century in the center of Paris.

Metropolitan Museum of Art New York's Met is the largest museum in the Western Hemisphere. Enough said.

State Hermitage Museum Six ornate baroque buildings on the banks of St. Petersburg's Neva river, housing the masterworks of many European painters: Rembrandt, Picasso, Van Gogh, and so on.

Visit an Oddball Museum

Museum of Failure "Learning is the only way to turn failure into success." That's the motto at this small museum in Helsingborg, Sweden, filled with innovation failures like the Apple Newton, Harley-Davidson perfume, Kodak digital cameras, and Google Glass.

Momofuku Ando Instant Ramen Museum Japanese museum in Osaka prefecture dedicated to Cup Noodles, the cheap and not-quite-healthy fuel for college students worldwide, invented here in 1958 by Momofuku Ando in his backyard workshop.

Museum of Jurassic Technology It's a cabinet of curiosities in Culver City, California. Some of the far-fetched exhibits are real, some are not. You decide which is which.

Museum of Bad Art (MOBA) Dedicated to the world's truly awful—as opposed to merely incompetent—landscapes and portraiture, with two permanent locations outside of Boston, Massachusetts.

Plastinarium Plastinated human bodies and organs showcasing the art of human dissection, about two hours from Berlin, Germany.

Go for a Swim

Bondi Icebergs The 50-meter saltwater pool overlooking Sydney's Bondi Beach has the best ocean views of any public pool, anywhere.

Gellért Baths Ornate indoor and outdoor pools in the heart of Budapest. Join the locals for a game of floating chess.

SkyPark The outdoor infinity pool at the Marina Bay Sands hotel is on the fifty-seventh floor in central Singapore. The skyline looks amazing.

Four Seasons Safari Lodge Swim in the Serengeti, in Tanzania, while watching elephants in an adjacent watering hole. It's surreal.

Piscine Molitor Paris's famous public pool complex now has a boutique hotel, an enclosed winter pool, and an outdoor summer pool with a real sand beach. Dress to impress.

Go Island Hopping

Palawan, Philippines Hiking, swimming, diving, an underground river, stunning limestone caverns—perfectly adventurous and the Philippines's answer to paradise. Not yet overcome by megaresorts.

Skopelos, Greece All the beauty of Santorini without the crowds. It's harder to reach (an hour by ferry from Skiathos), but that's part of Skopelos's charm.

Gili Trawangan, Indonesia What Bali was probably like back in the 1970s. No motorized vehicles, just hanging out with backpackers enjoying the sun and sea.

Malta Under-the-radar wonderfulness. Great food. Culture. History. Limestone cliffs. Baroque churches. Medieval castles and fortresses. What's not to like?!

Tasmania, Australia Miles of pristine coastal wilderness to explore. Fresh seafood, local wines, and just enough urban culture to keep things interesting. Oh yeah, and lots and lots of kangaroos.

Go Scuba Diving

Cocos Island, Costa Rica World's best diving with hammerhead sharks. Seriously. Liveaboards only.

Sipadan Island, Malaysia Barracuda Point, famous for coral, sharks, and massive schools of barracuda.

Big Island, Hawaii Manta ray night dives from Kona. Unforgettable.

Palau, Micronesia Blue Corner wall, upwelling with pelagic fish galore.

Raja Ampat, Indonesia More species of coral and fish than anywhere on the planet. Wild and remote archipelago. Liveaboards only.

Learn a New Talent

Film and TV School of the Academy of Performing Arts (FAMU) Enroll in Prague's acclaimed film school; roughly one hundred non-Czech students are accepted annually. FAMU alums include writer Milan Kundera (*The Unbearable Lightness of Being*) and director Miloš Forman (*Amadeus*).

La Viruta One of Buenos Aires's top tango clubs, and among the most accessible for foreigners of any skill level to take legitimate, professional tango lessons.

Codecademy Learn the basics of JavaScript, PHP, Python and other software development languages for free, at this well-respected online school.

New York Bartending School Learn the art of mixology at one of New York's top-rated bartending schools. Forty-hour certification courses cost around $800.

Witch School Interested in Wiccan, pagan, and magical esoterica? The online-only Witch School offers courses in symbolism, manifestation, and basic spell writing for witches and wizards in training.

Tour a Market or Bazaar

Tsukiji Fish Market The world's busiest fish market, on the outskirts of Tokyo. Most of the action happens before 7 A.M.

Marrakech Souk It takes a minimum of two days to explore the crowded alleyways and cramped stalls of Morocco's largest and liveliest marketplace.

Chatuchak Weekend Market Bangkok's massive outdoor market, worth a visit for the food and people watching as much as the goods for sale. Not to be confused with the equally awesome floating markets at Damnoen Saduak.

Grand Bazaar Istanbul's finest indoor bazaar for more than six centuries. Beyond the tourist-oriented shops, it's a wonderful warren of carpet shops and spice stalls.

Mercado San Juan de Dios Glorious traditional food, from fried goat to posole to fruit-filled empanadas, in a vast indoor marketplace in Guadalajara, Mexico.

Get a Massage

Wat Pho Part of the landmark temple complex in central Bangkok, Thailand, and the place for a traditional Thai massage for less than $15. Amazing. Massage classes also offered.

Cağaloğlu Hamam In Istanbul's Sultanahmet district, housed in an historic eighteenth-century Turkish bath with separate facilities for men and women. It's not relaxing—don't think "spa"—but the massage is an unforgettable (possibly harrowing?!) experience.

Centralbadet Indoor pool and relaxing oasis of calm in the otherwise busy city of Stockholm, Sweden. Try the "classic" (what the rest of the world calls "Swedish") massage.

Kusatsu Onsen Massive hot-spring resort, not far from Tokyo. It's famous for therapeutic waters and shiatsu, Japan's pressure-point style of massage.

Breitenbush Hot Springs Worker-owned co-op featuring holistic and spiritual retreats. The bucolic setting in rural southern Oregon is postcard-perfect.

Learn to Cook

Culinary Institute of America Take a five-day "cooking boot camp" aimed at novice chefs in St. Helena, the heart of northern California's wine country.

Los Dos Cooking School A low-cost, hugely popular cooking school dedicated to the cuisine of Mexico's Yucatán region, located in the Yucatán's capital city of Mérida.

North Carolina Barbecue Society A boot camp for barbecue lovers. Learn the secrets of pit masters for less than $500 at locations across North Carolina.

Way Cool Cooking School An award-winning, multidisciplinary school in Eden Prairie, Minnesota, aimed at kids ages seven to thirteen. Courses cost a few hundred dollars and last three to four days.

Ferrandi Paris In summer you can enroll in training weeks at one of Paris's top schools of culinary arts. Learn to make bread, pastries, and macaroons the way Parisians do.

Visit a Craft Brewery

Brewery Ommegang in Cooperstown, New York. A bucolic setting with great summer concerts and crisp American- and European-style (especially Belgian) ales.

Stone Brewing in Escondido, California, not far from San Diego. It's one of the most creative and award-winning craft breweries on the West Coast. The beer garden and restaurant are top notch.

Jester King Brewery, just outside of Austin, Texas. Unconventional ingredients and wild fermentation to make its ales and IPAs. Live music and the great outdoors complete the scene.

Baerlic Brewing in Portland, Oregon. Portland has more breweries than any other city in the world. Baerlic stands out for its single-hop IPAs and cream ales, and one of the city's coziest tasting rooms.

The Church Brew Works in Pittsburgh, Pennsylvania. It's inside a church, cool not kitschy, and the food is excellent.

Worship a Sports Stadium

Ryogoku Kokugikan Sumo Hall Catch a sumo tournament in Tokyo's national sumo hall. Tournaments run three times a year, for fifteen days each, in January, May, and September.

Croke Park Ireland's hallowed stadium is the place to catch the All-Ireland finals in Gaelic football and hurling, two of the world's most underappreciated sports.

Melbourne Cricket Ground The MCG hosts cricket, of course. It's also the spiritual home of Australian Rules Football, or footy. The footy season runs March through September.

The Float at Marina Bay It's an aptly named sports field floating in Singapore's Marina Bay. It doesn't matter which event you come to see, it's the stadium that grabs your attention and won't let go.

Fenway Park It's one of America's great quirky ballparks. It's also the league's fourth-smallest stadium and home to the Boston Red Sox.

Gamble in Style

Golden Nugget Las Vegas old-school gambling at its finest. The poker room is legendary.

Casino de Monte-Carlo It's one of the world's iconic casinos, and very much focused on high-rollers. It's in the wee country of Monaco, on France's southern border.

Kurhaus of Baden-Baden Elegance, luxury, charm—all with a nineteenth-century flair. Few casinos are as grand and opulent. It's in the German spa town of Baden-Baden.

Ritz Club London It's posh with a capital *P* and for members only. Guests staying at the equally posh Ritz hotel may enter, otherwise lifetime casino membership costs around $1,500.

The Cosmopolitan Sexy, stylish, and full of attitude, just the way Las Vegas likes it.

Play a Round of Golf

St. Andrews If you golf, you fantasize about playing the Old Course at St. Andrews, Scotland. It's been around since the late 1400s and is, without argument, the most famous golf course on the planet.

Pebble Beach Possibly the most famous course in the United States, and certainly the one with the finest ocean views from the eighteenth hole.

Augusta National Site of the Masters Tournament and home to golf's three most famously difficult holes: the eleventh, twelfth, and thirteenth.

Royal County Down Northern Ireland's most revered course, set between mountains and the Irish Sea just south of Belfast.

Shinnecock Hills One of the oldest courses in the United States, set in the lush countryside of Southampton, New York.

Expose Yourself to Public Art

Neon Museum Hundreds of casino neon signs from the 1950s and '60s are on display at the museum and adjacent outdoor Boneyard, just off the Las Vegas Strip.

Museo Subacuático de Arte (MUSA) It's an underwater contemporary art museum, just off Isla Mujeres near Cancun, Mexico. Snorkel or dive with full-scale statuary and designs. It's fantastic.

Memento Park The world's largest collection of Communist-era statuary, from Lenin and Marx to the "heroes" of Hungary's former Communist regime, located on the outskirts of central Budapest.

Park Güell Spanish architect Antoni Gaudí, famous for his wavy columns and multicolored ceramics, planned to transform a hillside into a garden-filled housing complex for the wealthy. The project was a flop and never completed. Today it's one of Barcelona's most worthwhile public parks.

Heidelberg Project A constantly evolving outdoor installation on the blighted east side of Detroit, Michigan. The art takes over entire sections of its namesake Heidelberg Street, calling attention to inner-city poverty.